WALKING
CHARLES DICKENS'
KENT

Published by Sigma Leisure – an imprint of
Sigma Press, Stobart House, Pontyclerc, Penybanc Road, Ammanford, Carmarthenshire SA18 3HP.

British Library Cataloguing in Publication Data
A CIP record for this book is available from the British Library.

ISBN: 978-1-910758-50-2

Typesetting and Design by: Sigma Press, Ammanford.

Cover photograph: Rochester Castle, seen from Minor Canon Row © Andy Bull

Photographs: © Andy Bull

Maps: Emily Duong

Printed by: Akcent Media

Disclaimer: the information in this book is given in good faith and is believed to be correct at the time of publication. No responsibility is accepted by either the author or publisher for errors or omissions, or for any loss or injury however caused. Only you can judge your own fitness, competence and experience. Do not rely solely on sketch maps for navigation: we strongly recommend the use of appropriate Ordnance Survey (or equivalent) maps.

WALKING CHARLES DICKENS' KENT

ANDY BULL

MAPS BY EMILY DUONG

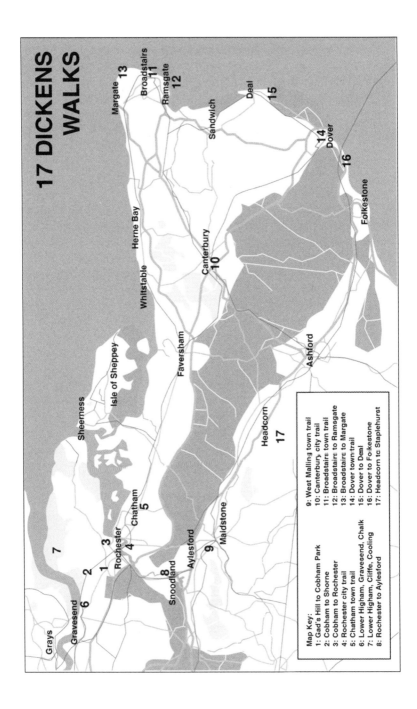

17 DICKENS WALKS

Grays
Gravesend
Sheerness
Isle of Sheppey
Rochester
Chatham
Snoodland
Aylesford
Maidstone
Headcorn
Whitstable
Herne Bay
Faversham
Canterbury
Ashford
Margate
Broadstairs
Ramsgate
Sandwich
Deal
Dover
Folkestone

1
2
3
4
5
6
7
8
9
10
11
12
13
14
15
16
17

Map Key:
1: Gad's Hill to Cobham Park
2: Cobham to Shorne
3: Cobham to Rochester
4: Rochester city trail
5: Chatham town trail
6: Lower Higham, Gravesend, Chalk
7: Lower Higham, Cliffe, Cooling
8: Rochester to Aylesford
9: West Malling town trail
10: Canterbury, city trail
11: Broadstairs town trail
12: Broadstairs to Ramsgate
13: Broadstairs to Margate
14: Dover town trail
15: Dover to Deal
16: Dover to Folkestone
17: Headcorn to Staplehurst

CONTENTS

INTRODUCTION

Kent meant more to Dickens than anywhere, after London, and he loved to walk it.

He wrote: 'My walking is of two kinds: one straight on and to a definite goal at a round pace; one objectless, loitering, and finely vagabond.'

In this spirit, the walks here are a mix of relaxed town and city trails and longer, focused treks through the countryside Dickens knew so well.

They include the last walk he ever took, his life-long favourite, through the parkland and woods of Cobham Hall. He walked it for the last time 150 years ago, on 7 June 1870, the day before being struck down by the brain haemorrhage that killed him. It was the very same walk he had sent his characters on in *The Pickwick Papers*, 25 years before, and it had never lost its appeal.

The walks gathered here are Dickens' best-loved, most frequently undertaken routes. They range from long hikes on the marshes that inspired *Great Expectations*, to ambles around the places of his childhood – Rochester and Chatham – which he first explored at the age of seven or eight, and which he went on to people with so many larger-than-life fictional characters in *The Pickwick Papers* and *The Mystery of Edwin Drood*.

There are also wonderful seaside hikes from the towns he spent his summers: Broadstairs, Dover and Folkestone, plus places he set his novels, stories and essays: the Canterbury of *David Copperfield*; the Deal of *Bleak House*; the Ramsgate from *Sketches by Boz*; and the many Kent locations in *The Uncommercial Traveller*. Along the way we stop at Dickens' favourite churches, pubs, hotels, picnic and resting places.

There is a saying, that, in order to truly understand someone, you must walk a mile in their shoes. In this book we walk many miles in Dickens' shoes, and gain true insights into his character, and a fuller understanding of his life, with its triumphs, challenges and tragedies.

I hope you will find that *Walking Charles Dickens' Kent* works both as a practical walker's companion – with outline maps, detailed route directions, places for refreshment and accommodation – and as an atmospheric armchair read. Each walk is introduced with an outline, rich with a range of references to events in Dickens' life and passages in his books that are directly relevant to the route to be followed.

The sights he saw on his walks and reproduced in his works: the landscapes, cities, towns, streets, churches, houses and rooms he encountered, are the very places we shall go. Along the way, thanks to William Hughes, who in 1891 published *A Week's Tramp in Dickens-Land*, we meet people who knew Dickens, and who share their recollections of him.

Many of the places that were of greatest significance to him are not generally open to the public, but we include details on how you can gain access to as many of them as possible.

HOW TO USE THIS BOOK

Each walk contains:
- An introduction to the route, exploring key places, and their factual and fictional connections with Dickens.
- What you need to know: essential information about the route and facilities along it
- An outline map of the route
- Step-by-step directions on following the route

Key places, labelled A, B, C etc, appear in the introduction, and those identifying letters recur in 'What you need to know', on the map, and within the step-by-step directions.

In an effort to ensure accuracy, each walk was recorded using GPS on the Ordnance Survey's mapping app. However, all distances should be treated as approximate. I recommend taking with you either the relevant OS Explorer paper map, or having the OS app open on your mobile device. I find the app invaluable, particularly when navigating complicated points along the way, and ensuring you do not go off your intended path.

The maps in this book were created by Emily Duong, building on open source mapping (c) OpenStreetMap contributors. Full licence conditions here: www.openstreetmap.org/copyright

A word of caution: conditions on the ground may change over time. Any essential updates will be listed at www.andybull.co.uk/dickenskent. If you find something that needs to be amended, I would be very grateful if you could let me know either on that website or via Twitter @andybull

Finally, at the back of the book, you will find a short biography of Charles Dickens, and reminders of the characters, and summaries of the plots, of the Dickens' books featured in these walks.

WALK 1: DICKENS' LAST WALK
GADS HILL AND COBHAM PARK CIRCUIT

Picture two beautiful days in June, thirty-four years apart. On the first, Charles Dickens' characters in *The Pickwick Papers* are taking a jolly amble along what was their creator's favourite walk. On the second, we see Dickens himself, the day before his fatal brain haemorrhage, following the very same route through the woods and across the park at Cobham Hall for the very last time. Just forty-eight hours later, on 9 June 1870, the most famous man of the Victorian age would be dead.

No other walk, and no other location, can bring us closer, or reveal as much, about Charles Dickens. We will set out from the only house he ever owned, where he lived for 13 years, and where he died. **Gad's Hill Place (A)** is set back behind majestic cedars on the old London to Dover Road at Higham, 7km (4 miles) east of Rochester. (See 'What you need to know' to arrange a tour)

Dickens had dreamed of owning Gad's Hill since childhood. His father often pointed out the house as they passed, later inspiring a nostalgic essay in *The Uncommercial Traveller*, written there. In it, Dickens imagines meeting himself as a small boy at this spot, and his two personas gazing together at 'the house at the top of the hill'. The boy says: 'ever since I can recollect, my father, seeing me so fond of it, has often said to me, "If you were to be very persevering and were to work hard, you might some day come to live in it".'

In 1856, Dickens discovered the house was for sale, and bought it. He had the place renovated and moved in the following year. Here, he wrote *Little Dorrit*, *A Tale of Two Cities*, *Great Expectations*, *Our Mutual Friend*, and the final, unfinished, *The Mystery of Edwin Drood*, which he was working on the day after his last walk. According to Dickens' great-granddaughter Monica Dickens, 'here he learned to love the countryside as much as he loved London'.

Gad's Hill occupied a life-long place in Dickens' imagination, and entered his fiction long before he bought it. David Copperfield walks past this house on his long trek from London to Dover. In *A Christmas Carol*, when the Spirit of Christmas Past takes Scrooge to the scenes of his childhood, it is here that the spirit brings him: to 'a mansion of dull red brick, with a little weathercock-surmounted cupola on the roof, and a bell hanging in it'.

If you visit the house today, you can look up the stairwell and see the rope which rang that bell. The house remains redolent of Dickens, despite having

Gad's Hill Place, the house Dickens dreamed of owning as a child, and lived in for his last 13 years

been a school since 1924. The banisters on the curving staircase bear the stencilled decorations applied by his daughter, Katey. The horseshoe Dickens placed on the stairs, inverted to let good luck flow out into the house, is still there. The large hall cupboard concealing the dumb waiter, with which food was brought up from the basement kitchens, is still here and in working order.

To reach the hallway you will have passed through the porch, flanked with painted benches which, Dickens used to claim, were made from furniture that once belonged to Shakespeare. Here, his dogs Linda, a St Bernard, and Turk, a Mastiff, would have been tethered on long chains to ward off passing tramps and thieves.

The first room off the hall on the right was Dickens' study. Inset into the panelling on either side of the bay window, in which a replica of Dickens' desk stands, are tall, slim mirrors in which he would watch himself as he acted out the episode he was writing.

On the back of the door are false book spines with the joke titles he created: *Cats' Lives* (in nine volumes); *King Henry the Eighth's Evidences of Christianity* (five volumes); *History of a Short Chancery Suit* (21 volumes); and *Hansard's Guide to Refreshing Sleep* (many volumes).

Across the hall from the study is the drawing room where Dickens, who loved light, placed large mirrors on the walls to reflect the natural light coming in from the window at the front of the house. This was where the family and guests would gather each evening; Dickens often standing at a custom-built lectern to read from work in progress.

At the far end of the room, the bay window has been adapted to create a sort of stable door giving direct access to the grand conservatory he had built along the back of the house shortly before he died. You push up the sash window and the panelling beneath opens to let you duck your head and walk through.

Dickens sat with his sister-in-law and housekeeper Georgina Hogarth in the conservatory, gauging the effect of some Chinese lanterns he had just bought, on the evening after his final walk. The conservatory connects with the dining room, and it is here that Dickens suffered his fatal seizure at 6pm on June 8, 1870. A chaise similar to the one that servants lifted his unconscious form on to after his seizure stands on the spot, to the left of the door leading out into the hall.

Dickens adored this house. From it he could gaze over the landscapes that meant most to him, which suffuse his writing, and where he loved to walk. To the east he could make out historic Rochester, where his imagination first sparked into life. Just beyond it was smoky, grimy Chatham, where he spent idyllic early years before an uncertain, scarring childhood. To the west was London, the city he understood so well, and whose grim underbelly he forced his vast audience to comprehend. North were the low flat marshes of the Thames Estuary, where he set *Great Expectations*. To the south east was Bluebell Hill, a favourite picnic spot and, due south, the long undulating line of woods and park at Cobham, and the course of that favourite, final walk.

In the front garden, a tunnel leads beneath the road to an area of land sheltered by cedars which Dickens called The Wilderness. Here stood a two-storey Swiss chalet where he wrote in good weather. The tunnel allowed the man who was perhaps the first superstar to get to his work without being troubled by inquisitive fans. The chalet is now in Rochester, and can be seen on Walk 4. Under one of the cedars is the grave of his favourite St Bernard, 'the big and beautiful Linda'.

In a letter, Dickens wrote of the chalet, where he spent his last full day alive: 'Diverse birds sing here all day, and the nightingales all night. The place is lovely and in perfect order... I have put five mirrors in the chalet where I write, and they reflect and refract, in all kinds of ways, the leaves that are quivering at the windows, and the great fields of waving corn, and the sail-dotted river. My room is up among the branches of the trees; and the birds and the butterflies fly in and out, and the green branches shoot in at the open windows, and the lights and shadows of the clouds come and go with the rest of the company. The scent of the flowers, and indeed of everything that is growing for miles and miles, is most delicious.'

But Gad's Hill Place was by no means an exclusively happy place. It was also the house Dickens moved to shortly after abandoning his wife, Catherine, claiming she did not love him, that she wanted a separation, and was suffering from a mental disorder, none of which was true. His children were ordered to stay with him. Only the eldest, Charley, defied him and sided with his mother. Dickens' besotted sister-in-law, Georgina, clung to him, keeping house. Meanwhile he conducted a clandestine affair with Ellen Ternan, a young actress – 18 to his 45 – known as Nelly.

This was also the place where Dickens worked himself to death, aged just 58.

Let's leave the house and follow in Dickens' footsteps as he takes that final walk.

The passageway beneath the road between Gad's Hill Place which enabled Dickens to get to his writing chalet unobserved

Down Crutches Lane beside the house, skirting Great Crabbles Wood, we enter the **woods and parkland (B)** of Cobham Hall. Here we are stepping into the pages of The Pickwick Papers, and following in the footsteps of Samuel Pickwick and his companions.

Dickens writes: 'A delightful walk it was; for it was a pleasant afternoon in June, and their way lay though a deep and shady wood, cooled by the light wind which gently rustled rather thick foliage, and enlivened by the songs of the birds that perched upon the boughs. The ivy and the moss crept in thick clusters over the old trees, and the soft green turf overspread the ground like a silken mat. They emerged upon an open park, with an ancient hall, displaying the quaint and picturesque architecture of Elizabeth's time. Long vistas of stately oaks and elm trees appeared on every side: large herds of deer were cropping the fresh grass; and occasionally a startled hare scoured along the ground with the speed of the shadows thrown by the light clouds, which swept across a sunny landscape like a passing breath of summer.'

On Dickens' final walk here, in the afternoon of 7 June 1870, it was a mark of how exhausted he was that he had his carriage take him and Georgina Hogarth down to Cobham Hall, where he got down to walk alone through the woods and park back to Gad's Hill.

Along the way he will have passed a ghoulish spot that he relished. **Dadd's Hole (C)**, a little way up Richard Dadd Path, and off to the right, is where, in 1843, the artist Richard Dadd murdered his father, Robert. It was a brutal slaying, and one which fascinated Dickens. When he brought guests on this walk he would often pause at the spot, recounting the details of the murder.

Edmund Yates, who stayed at Gad's Hill Place in the 1860s, said: 'Dickens acted out the whole scene with his usual dramatic force.' Another, William

Richard Dadd's Path leads past a notorious murder spot where Dickens loved to act out the crime for fellow walkers

Frith, who had been a close friend of Richard Dadd, and a fellow member of a group of artists known as the Clique, wrote, of how 'Dickens was eloquent on the subject of the Dadd parricide, showing us the place where the body was found, with many startling and interesting details of the discovery.' This must have been chilling for Frith. After Dadd's incarceration in Bethlem, England's first mental institution, a search of his studio found portraits of Frith, and other members of the Clique, with their throats cut.

Cobham Hall (D), was owned by Dickens' great friend, the Earl of Darnley. (See 'What you need to know' to arrange a visit). In Dickens' time the house, which has two long Tudor wings connected by a central section designed by Inigo Jones, held one of the finest private art collections in the world, with works by Titian, Rubens, Van Dyck and Joshua Reynolds. The ornate galleried music-room, which you will see if you tour the house, was said by George IV to be the finest room in England.

You might like to end your walk across the road from Gad's Hill Place, in the **Sir John Falstaff pub (E).** Dickens stayed here while his house was being renovated, and guests including Wilkie Collins, author of *The Woman In White*, lodged here when Gad's Hill was full. Another reason Dickens loved this spot was that it was once a notoriously dangerous place favoured by highwaymen. In *Henry IV Part I*, Shakespeare has Prince Hal and Poins trick Falstaff into

The Sir John Falstaff, across the road from Gad's Hill Place and Dickens' local

robbing a rich pilgrim at Gad's Hill and then, in disguise, relieve him of his ill-gotten gains.

Dickens wrote: 'The robbery was committed before the door, on the ground now covered by the room in which I write. A little rustic alehouse, called the Sir John Falstaff, is over the way, has been over the way ever since, in honour of the event.'

The pub remains very much the friendly local Dickens knew. He was great friends with the landlord, William Trood, whose surname echoes that of Edwin Drood, central character in his final novel.

William Hughes, author of *A Week's Tramp in Dickens-Land*, chatted with the landlord in 1891, and wrote: 'Mr Trood sometimes acted as local banker to Charles Dickens, and used to cash his cheques for him. Only the day before his death, he cashed a cheque for £22, and was subsequently offered £24 for it by an admirer of Dickens who desired the autograph; but to his credit it should be mentioned that he did not accept the offer.'

That cheque has led to a suspicion of a cover-up regarding Dickens' final hours. When he died, only £6.6s.3d remained. How had he spent the then substantial sum of £15.13s.9d in just a few hours? Claire Tomalin, in *Charles Dickens: A Life*, recounts the 'wild, improbable but not entirely impossible' theory, that on the morning of June 8, he may have gone to visit his mistress Ellen Ternan at her house in Peckham, and suffered his seizure there, being brought back, in secret and unconscious, to Gad's Hill in a big two-horse brougham to avoid a scandal.

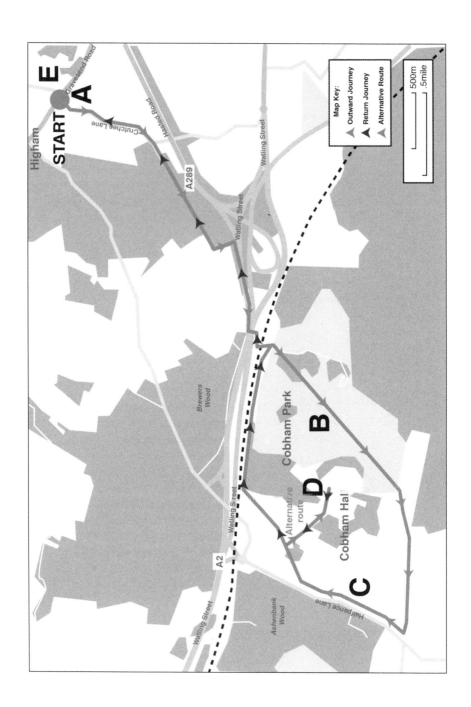

THE WALK

What you need to know	
Distance	11.8km/7.3miles
Time	3 hours (not including stops)
Terrain	Gentle descent on outward journey, through woodland and over grass after initial 500m/550yds on road (no pavement but traffic generally light). Gentle ascent on return over same mix of terrain
Map	OS Explorer 163 Gravesend & Rochester
Starting point	Gad's Hill Place, Gravesend Rd, Higham, Rochester ME3 7PA
How to get there	Car, or train to Higham station (1.6km/1mile from start of walk)
Key points along the way	Gad's Hill Place (A on map). To book a tour of Gad's Hill Place go to www.visitgravesend.co.uk/whats-on/tours-gads-hill-place or phone 01474 337600 Thursday to Sunday only. Cobham Hall (D on map). To arrange to visit Cobham Hall go to www.cobhamhall.com/427/open-to-the-public
Refreshments	The Sir John Falstaff, Gravesend Rd, Higham, Rochester ME3 7DZ. 01634 717104

Step-by-step directions

Take Crutches Lane beside Gad's Hill School (A) and follow it downhill. After 600m/660yds, as the road bends left, a footpath goes off to the right into Great Crabbles Wood.

Follow the path, keeping the fence to your left, for 700m/765yds, where there are two stiles in quick succession. The second leads to a narrow, tarmacked track. Turn left.

After 100m/110yds, when this path ends in a T junction, turn right onto another tarmacked track.

After 500m/550yds you arrive at a bridge over the A2. Turn left to cross the road then go through the tunnel under the railway.

In 20m/22yds, ignore footpaths to right and left. Go straight on until, after another 20m/22yds, you see a footpath sign on your right before the entrance to the golf club.

Follow the footpath through the woods to the golf course. You are now in Cobham Park (B). Take care crossing the fairways, following the line of posts bearing yellow footpath markers that run straight ahead across the course.

When you reach a footpath crossing your path, turn right and follow it to a belt of trees at the edge of the course. You will have views of Cobham Hall through trees to the right. The distance across the course is 1.5km/.9mile.

You come out into Lodge Lane. Turn right. In 600m/660yds you reach Halfpence Lane, at the edge of Cobham village.

On the grassy bank to your right at this junction is a sign pointing left to Richard Dadd's Path. The path runs parallel with Halfpence Lane along the edge of the field, with a hedge between you and the road.

After about 100m/110yds, and 50m/55yds to your right in the meadow, is Dadd's Hole (C), a couple of small bushy trees with a fence encircling them.

In 1km/.6miles at the end of Richard Dadd's Path turn right, skirt the pond and head for a point on the left-hand corner of the small copse across the meadow. There is a silver-painted stile at this point, but pass to the left of it, heading for the two black stiles on either side of the drive ahead of you.

If you are going to Cobham Hall (D) on an open day, turn right on this drive to the house, and retrace your steps after your visit to re-join this path.

Once across the drive, keep straight ahead over the field, using the post on the brow of the field as a guide. When, after 500m/550yds, you reach a fence enclosing an angling pond, turn left towards the railway, go through the silver stile and follow the path that runs alongside the railway tracks for 1km/.6miles.

When you reach a lane you have gone full circle. Turn left, retracing your steps under the railway and over the motorway. Turn right and follow the track alongside the A2 for 500m/550yds until, after passing between two large tree trunks placed to restrict the path, take the left turn.

After passing through a small wood, take the stile on the right, and follow the path on the edge of the wood for 700m/770yds.

When you reach Crutches Lane, turn left and walk 600m/660yds to Gad's Hill and our starting point. The Sir John Falstaff (E) is diagonally right across the road.

Walk 2: Dickens' favourite villages
Cobham and Shorne circuit

Cobham was Dickens' favourite village, and contains his favourite pub, the Leather Bottle. He would often stay here in the years before he bought Gad's Hill Place at nearby Higham, and visited it regularly with friends once he was living there. He also loved the neighbouring village of Shorne, and this walk takes in both.

Dickens' son Charley wrote of his father's interest in Cobham: 'he never wearied of acting as cicerone [guide] to his guests to its fine church and the quaint almshouses with the disused refectory behind it.' Not to mention the Leather Bottle. Dickens first stayed here in 1841, returning many times before he moved to the area in 1857.

In *The Pickwick Papers*, Dickens' first novel, Cobham plays a key role. Samuel Pickwick and companions come here in pursuit of one of their number, the love-lorn Tracy Tupman, who has sought solace in

The Leather Bottle, Cobham, which Dickens visited many times and which appears in *The Pickwick Papers*

Cobham after the maiden aunt he was wooing at Dingley Dell eloped with the slippery actor Alfred Jingle. Tupman slipped away from Dingley Dell, the model for which we visit on Walk 8, apparently deeply depressed. He left an ominous note reading: 'Any letter addressed to me at the Leather Bottle, Cobham, Kent, will be forwarded – supposing I still exist.'

As Samuel Pickwick and friends approach Cobham on a sparkling June day, Dickens writes: '"If this," said Mr Pickwick, looking about him, "if this were the place to which all who are troubled with our friend's complaint came, I fancy their old attachment to this world would very soon return... for a misanthrope's choice, this is one of the prettiest and most desirable places of residence I ever met with."'

At the **Leather Bottle (A)** they find 'a clean and commodious village ale-house... the parlour... a long, low-roofed room, furnished with a large number of high-backed leather-cushioned chairs, of fantastic shapes, and embellished with a great variety of old portraits, and roughly-coloured prints of some antiquity. At the upper end of the room was a table, with a white cloth upon it, well covered with a roast fowl, bacon, ale, and etceteras; and at the table sat Mr Tupman, looking as unlike a man who had taken his leave of the world, as possible.'

The Leather Bottle is still an unpretentious village inn, where the connection with the author is cherished. The bar where Tupman was discovered is now the Dickens Room. An extensive collection of illustrations, and memorabilia – including a single hair from Dickens' head and the leather bag he took on his first reading tour – is found throughout the public areas, and Dickens' novels are placed in the bedrooms.

After Tupman has eaten his feast, and Pickwick 'having refreshed himself with a copious draught of ale' the pair cross the street to the church where: 'For half an hour, their forms might have been seen pacing the churchyard to and fro, while Mr Pickwick was engaged in combating his companion's resolution... Whether Mr Tupman was already tired of retirement, or whether he was wholly unable to resist the eloquent appeal which was made to him, matters not, he did not resist it at last ... Mr Pickwick smiled; they shook hands, and walked back to rejoin their companions.'

The lovely old church of **St Mary Magdalen (B)** has reputedly the finest collection of monumental brasses in the world dating from 1300 to 1529. Tucked behind the church is **The New College of Cobham (C),** which dates from the thirteenth century and which was another of Dickens' favourite places. (See 'What you need to know' below for details on visiting both.)

A description of Cobham churchyard at another time of year, Christmas, appears in Dickens' tale *The Seven Poor Travellers*: 'the mists

New College Cobham, now an alms house

began to rise in the most beautiful manner, and the sun to shine; and as I went on through the bracing air, seeing the hoar-frost sparkle everywhere, I felt as if all Nature shared in the joy of the great Birthday... I came to the village, and the churchyard where the dead had been quietly buried "in the sure and certain hope" which Christmastide inspired.'

From 1362 until its dissolution at the Reformation, The New College of Cobham was home to five priests. It was founded by Sir John de Cobham, whose family lived in Cobham Hall at the time.

This was a chantry house, in which the priests prayed and held regular intercessory masses for their benefactors, the Cobhams, and for Edward III, who granted Cobham a licence to establish the college, and for his wife, Queen Phillipa. They prayed for their well-being during their lives and, after their deaths, for their souls, and for the souls of their ancestors and heirs.

After its closure on Henry VIII's orders in 1537, the building was abandoned until 1597 when it was converted, by the tenth Lord Cobham, into an almshouse and given its present name. It still houses the poor of the parish.

Leaving Cobham, our walk takes us to another of Dickens' favourite villages, and uses a familiar route of his between the two, along ancient byways and through Shorne Woods. As John Forster, Dickens' friend and first biographer says: 'for a shorter summer walk, he was... fond of going round the village of Shorne, and sitting on a hot afternoon in its pretty shaded churchyard.'

This church, **St Peter and St Paul (D)**, was almost Dickens's final resting place. When his son Charley and son-in-law Charles Collins were seeking to fulfil his wish for a quiet burial in a place he loved, they approached the vicar here, and it was agreed he should be buried on the eastern side of the churchyard. The plan was abandoned in the face of national demands that he be buried in Westminster Abbey.

William Hughes, author, in 1891, of *A Week's Tramp in Dickens-Land*, believes Dickens was probably

St Peter and St Paul, Shorne, where Dickens was to have been buried

thinking of this spot when, in *The Pickwick Papers*, he describes: 'one of the most peaceful and secluded churchyards in Kent, where wild flowers mingle with the grass, and the soft landscape around, forms the fairest spot in the garden of England'.

It certainly makes a very pleasant spot to rest before the walk back to Cobham, as does Shorne's pub, the **Rose and Crown (E)** another hostelry that Dickens knew well.

THE WALK

What you need to know	
Distance	11.7km/7.3miles
Time	3 hours (not including stops)
Terrain	Gentle climb throughout outward journey, initially along a quiet lane and then through woodland. Gentle ascent on return, initially via another quiet lane, then through woodland
Map	OS Explorer 163 Gravesend & Rochester
Starting point	Leather Bottle, Cobham DA12 3BZ
How to get there	Car to Cobham (a car park is signed in the village) or train to Sole Street, which is 1.6km/1mile south west of Cobham
Key points along the way	St. Mary Magdalen, Cobham (B on the map) The church is open every day: www.cobham-luddesdowne.org The New College of Cobham (C on the map) The public areas of the almshouses are open April to September daily, 10am to 7pm, and from October to March, 10am to 4pm
Refreshments and accommodation	The Rose and Crown, Shorne (E on the map), for drink and food. www.roseandcrownatshorne.co.uk 01474 822373

Step-by-step directions

Across The Street from the Leather Bottle (A) is St. Mary Magdalen (B) and, behind the church, The New College of Cobham (C).

After visiting them, return to The Street, turn left and walk for 200m/220yds. Turn right into Battle St.

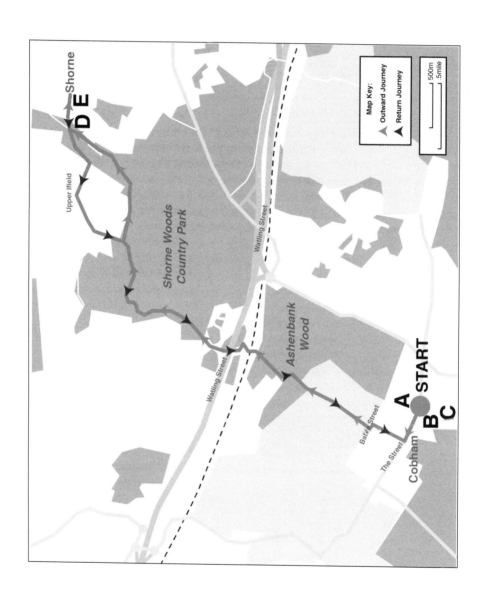

After 300m/330yds, at the end of Battle St, follow the sunken lane between hedges as it swings left and then right.

After 1.3km/.8miles you will reach a tarmacked lane and cross the railway lines before reaching a tarmacked road where you turn left and cross the A2.

After the entrance to the Inn on the Lake hotel, take the footpath to the right of the road that goes into Shorne Wood.

[There are numerous waymarked trails crisscrossing Shorne Wood. If you miss your path, you need to reach the wood's north eastern point to exit for Shorne.] After 1.2km/.75miles follow the track as it turns right.

After a further 400m/440yds, ignore the track to the left signposted to Shorne Ifield Road and keep straight on.

For 700m/770yds the track runs near the fringe of the wood, with open fields and glimpses of the wonderful view down to the Medway and Essex to your left.

After 800m/880yds you will reach a lane, Shorne Ifield Road. Turn right.

After 100m/110yds, take Butcher's Hill, the path on your right that runs downhill between brick walls. The church of St Peter and St Paul (D) is on your right.

A further 30m/33yds brings you to The Street where, if you turn right, you will reach the Rose and Crown (E) pub after a few metres.

To return to Cobham:

Turn left out of the Rose and Crown and, after a few metres, take Butcher's Hill, the path running uphill between brick walls.

When you reach a lane, Shorne Ifield Road, turn left.

Follow the lane (which has very little traffic on it) for 700m/770yds, then take the footpath to your left back into Shorne Woods.

After 200m/220yds, at a T-junction of paths, turn right.

You are now retracing your steps all the way back to Cobham.

After 400m/440yds, turn left on the path that runs south.

Follow this path for 500m/550yds until you reach a sign that points right and reads 'Exit to Thong Lane and A2'. Follow this path.

After 400m/440yds you reach Thong Lane. Turn left and follow the lane over the A2.

Turn right onto the narrow lane that takes you over the railway line and leads to the byway back to Cobham.

After 500m/550yds, where the path divides, take the left fork.

After 800m/880yds the route becomes tarmacked. Take the right fork and walk 300m/330yds down Battle Street to the main road (The Street) through Cobham.

Turn left to arrive at the Leather Bottle after 200m/220yds.

Walk 3: A walk with Dickens' father and Mr Pickwick

Cobham to Rochester

This is a route for really enjoying the country Dickens loved, and comes with two options: a long route to Rochester, and a much shorter circuit through Cobham Park.

The full route follows the Long Walk from Cobham to Rochester and back, which Dickens often took as a child, with his father. It is the same path which Samuel Pickwick and friends take on their approach to Cobham Park in *The Pickwick Papers*.

The Pickwickians walk to Cobham in pursuit of one of their number, the love-lorn Tracy Tupman, who has sought solace there after the maiden aunt he was wooing at Dingley Dell eloped with the slippery actor Alfred Jingle. There is more on that topic in Walk 2.

Once Dickens was living at Gad's Hill Place, from 1857, his direct route to Rochester would have been down the old Dover Road. However, as today this is very busy, and there are no convenient footpaths following its route, The Long Walk offers the best way to make the journey.

If you prefer, a quick return trip can be made by rail to Sole Street station, 1.6km/1mile from Cobham, which opens the possibility of following Walk 4: Rochester city trail, before your return.

There is also a shorter circular route through Cobham Park, marked as alternative route on the map.

The route is high on atmosphere but relatively light on Dickens-related locations. On both routes you pass **The Darnley Mausoleum (A)**. Dickens was a great friend of the 8th Earl Darnley, who owned Cobham Hall, and whose ancestor, the 3rd Earl, had this monumental pyramid mausoleum built in 1786 to house his ancestors. It never did, possibly because the Bishop of Rochester refused to consecrate it.

Dickens had a key to the parkland we walk through today, so he could come here whenever he liked. Today the Great Wood, which we pass through, is in the care of the National Trust, who have introduced cattle to keep the vegetation in check.

On the long route you pass a pub with great Dickens connections. The **Crispin and Crispianus (B)** in Strood High Street was a frequent refreshment

The Darnley Mausoleum: built to house the remains of the ancestors of the owner of Cobham Hall, but never used

point for Dickens on his way to and from Rochester, and he mentions it in *The Uncommercial Traveller*.

William Hughes, in his 1891 guide, *A Week's Tramp In Dickens-Land*, met the landlady, who remembered Dickens well. He writes: 'Mrs Masters, whose recollections of Dickens are very vivid, said: 'Lor! We never thought much about him when he was alive; it was only when his death took place that we understood what a great man he was.'

Mrs Masters gives Hughes a wonderfully detailed picture of Dickens the walker. She 'describes Dickens to us (as we sit in the seat he used now and then to occupy), when on one of his walks, as habituated in low shoes not over-well mended, loose large check-patterned trousers that sometimes got entangled in the shoes when walking, a brown coat thrown open, sometimes without a waistcoat, a belt instead of braces, a necktie which now and then got round towards his ear, and a large-brimmed felt hat, similar to an American's, set well at the back of his head.

'In his hand he carried by the middle an umbrella, which he was in the habit of constantly swinging, and if he had dogs (not an infrequent occurrence), he had a small whip as well. He walked in the middle of the road at a rapid pace, upright, but with his eyes cast down as if in deep thoughts.

'When he called at the Crispin for refreshment, usually a glass of ale, or a little cold brandy and water, he walked straight in, and sat down at the corner of the settle on the right-hand side where the arm is, opposite the fire-place; he rarely spoke to anyone, but looked round as though taking in everything at a glance.'

Mrs Masters also had a tale of Dickens' humanity. Hughes writes: 'Once he and a friend were

The Crispin and Crispianus, in Strood High Street, was one of Dickens' favourite stopping place on his frequent walks to Rochester

sheltering during a storm, and while Dickens stood looking out of the window he saw opposite a poor woman with a baby, who appeared very worn, wet, and travel-stained. She too was sheltering from the rain.

'"Call her in here," said Dickens. Mrs Masters obeyed. Dickens told her to draw the woman some brandy and she drank it. Dickens gave her a shilling, and remarked to Mrs Masters that "now she will go on her way rejoicing".'

Dickens mentions this pub, and the route we have taken to get here, in a chapter on tramps in *The Uncommercial Traveller*. At the time, the term tramp was used to cover the many, often highly-skilled, classes of itinerant worker who travelled the country to make their living. In it he imagines himself as a travelling clock-maker who has just serviced the turret stable clock at Cobham Hall.

He writes: 'Our task at length accomplished, we should be taken into an enormous servants' hall, and there regaled with beef and bread and powerful ale. Then paid freely we should be at liberty to go, and should be told by a pointing helper to keep round over yinder by the blasted ash, and so straight through the woods, till we should see the town lights right afore us. So should we lie that night at the ancient sign of the Crispin and Crispanus, and rise early next morning to be betimes on tramp again.'

Sadly, at the time of writing the pub is closed, but there are periodic moves to have it renovated and reopened. It would be a wonderful addition to the area's Dickens attractions if it were.

THE WALK

What you need to know	
Distance	Full circuit Cobham to Rochester: 16.7km/10.4miles Alternative circuit through Cobham Park: 5.2km/3.25miles
Time	Full circuit: 3 hours 15 minutes (not including stops) Alternative circuit through Cobham Park: 1 hour 15 minutes (not including stops)
Terrain	Full circuit: Well-maintained paths, gently undulating on first half of walk through woodland, then a steady descent on pavements through the Rochester suburbs to the city. Return journey the reverse of this. Alternative circuit through Cobham Park: Well-maintained paths through woods and over grass
Map	OS Explorer 163 Gravesend & Rochester
Starting point	Car Park off The Street, Cobham
How to get there	Car to Cobham or train to Sole Street, which is 1.6km/1mile from Cobham. Returning from Rochester by retracing steps, or via train to Sole Street
Key points along the way	The Darnley Mausoleum (A on the map) is generally open one day a week. For details: www.nationaltrust.org.uk/cobham-wood-and-mausoleum
Refreshments and accommodation	Cobham: The Leather Bottle (drink, food, accommodation) www.theleatherbottle.pub. 01474 814327. The Darnley Arms (drink, food, accommodation) 01474 814218. The Ship Inn (drink, food) www.greeneking-pubs.co.uk/pubs/kent/ship-inn/ 01474 814326 Rochester: Numerous pubs and restaurants

Step-by-step directions

Outward route

From The Street in Cobham, walk east. Where Halfpence Lane runs off to the left, walk straight ahead on Lodge Lane. After 700m/770yds the road becomes a track running through the Deer Park. The route is clearly marked and easy to follow, passing the Darnley Mausoleum (A) after 2km/1.25miles.

[The short route leaves this route shortly after the mausoleum. For directions on it, see 'Alternative route' below]

After a further 2.5km/1.6miles the path takes you over a railway and then under a motorway. You emerge on the edge of Rochester in Razorbill Close. When that road meets Albatross Avenue after 50m/55yds, turn left.

After a further 50m/55yds turn right where Albatross Avenue meets Bligh Way.

Follow Bligh Way for 1km/.6miles until it meets Darnley Road.

Follow Darnley Road for 1.4km/.9miles until you reach Northcote Road, on your left. Turn into Northcote Road.

At the end of Northcote turn right into the High Street, A2. Across the street. After 50m/55yds you reach the Crispin and Crispianus pub (B).

Follow the High Street for 800m/880yds until it crosses Rochester Bridge over the

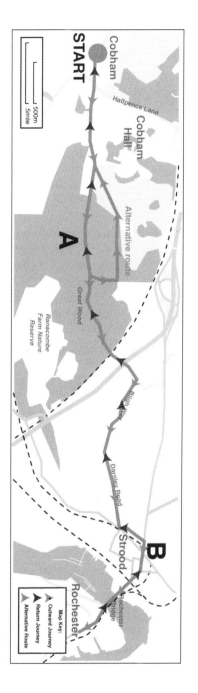

Medway. If you are returning by rail, Rochester railway station is on your left after 400m/440yds

Return route
Return over Rochester Bridge, then follow the High Street for 800m/880yds.

Turn left into Northcote Road. At the end of Northcote Road is Darnley Road.

Turn right into Darnley Road.

Follow Darnley Road for 1.4km/.9miles until it becomes Bligh Way.

Continue along Bligh Way for 1km/.6miles until you reach Albatross Avenue.

Turn left into Albatross Avenue, then right into Razorbill Close.

Pass under the motorway and over the railway, emerging in woodland.

Follow the path for 2.5km/1.6miles, where you pass Darnley Mausoleum.

Continue for 2km/1.25miles, where the track becomes Lodge Lane.

Continue on Lodge Lane for 700m/770yds until you reach The Street.

Continue straight on for Cobham village.

Alternative route
400m/440yds after passing Darnley Mausoleum you reach a crossroads. Turn left, walking over the golf course for 400m/440yds until another path crosses yours. Turn left and follow this path back towards Cobham, re-joining Lodge Lane after 1.4km/.9miles. Turn right to return to your starting point in Cobham.

Walk 4: The 'birthplace of his fancy'
Rochester city trail

Rochester meant more to Dickens than anywhere else in Kent. He knew it intimately as a child, in early adulthood he visited regularly, and he returned permanently in middle age, when he bought Gad's Hill Place at Higham, three miles away.

John Forster, friend and biographer, said that Rochester was 'the birth-place of his fancy'. It's clear that the city, and the memories associated with it, inspired him enormously throughout his career.

Rochester is the most important setting in his first, sparkling, fun-filled novel, *The Pickwick Papers*. It plays a central role, as Our Town, in *Great Expectations*; Dickens' tale of Pip, the orphan who becomes elevated to the role of a moneyed young gentleman thanks to an anonymous benefactor. The city shows another, darker side in the haunting, unfinished final work, *The Mystery of Edwin Drood*, where it is known as Cloisterham.

Rochester is also the location of an intriguing coincidence in Dickens' own life, relating to Ellen Ternan, his mistress for 13 years.

Several Rochester landmarks recur in Dickens' fiction, including **The Royal Victoria and Bull Inn (A)**. The Pickwickians, Pip and Dickens himself all used what was once the finest hotel in the city ('Good house – nice beds' Alfred Jingle says of it in *Pickwick*) but which is now awaiting renovation.

You will have to imagine the central archway into the courtyard as it was in 1827, when the Pickwickians found 'haunches of venison, saddles of mutton, ribs of beef, York hams, fowls and ducks, hang over our heads in the capacious covered gateway.'

To the left of the archway was the coffee room where, in *Pickwick*, Dr Slammer has Nathaniel Winkle challenged to a duel, mistaking him for Jingle, who had cut in on a lady the doctor was dancing with in the hotel ballroom.

The ballroom occupied the first floor to the back of the hotel. Dickens wrote: 'It was a long room, with crimson-covered benches, and wax candles in glass chandeliers. The musicians were securely confined in an elevated den, and quadrilles were being systematically got through by two or three sets of dancers.'

Dickens often stayed at the hotel, in Room 17, and he gave that room to Mr Pickwick, and to Pip, when his expectations were high.

In *Great Expectations* the Bull (it only became The Royal Victoria and Bull in 1901) is disguised as the Blue Boar, not to be confused with an actual Blue Boar further down the High Street towards Chatham. Dickens sets key passages in the novel here. Pip celebrates being apprenticed to the blacksmith Joe Gargery at the hotel. Later, it is where Pip and Bentley Drummle, standing shoulder to shoulder against the fireplace, almost come to blows as rivals for the hand of Miss Havisham's ward, the ice-cold Estella.

Finally, once Pip's mysterious patron is revealed to be the convict Magwitch, and Pip's fortune is lost, he looks out of the coffee room window and reflects bitterly that: 'Whereas the Boar had cultivated my good opinion with warm assiduity when I was coming into property, the Boar was exceedingly cool on the subject now that I was going out of property.'

Our next stopping point, **Rochester Bridge (B)** features in *Pickwick*, *Great Expectations* and *Edwin Drood*. Mr Pickwick comes here before breakfast at the Bull, and looks out at a far more rural scene than we see today: 'On either side, the banks of the Medway, covered with cornfields and pastures, with here and there a windmill, or a distant church, stretched away as far as the eye could see... The river, reflecting the clear blue of the sky, glistened and sparkled as it flowed noiselessly on; and the oars of the fishermen dipped into the water with a clear and liquid sound, as their heavy but picturesque boats glided slowly down the stream.'

In *Great Expectations*, the bridge is the scene of comic humiliation for Pip when, dressed in his finery and about to set off for his new life in London, he is pursued by the tailor Trabb's boy: 'passing abreast of me, he pulled up his shirt-collar, twined his side hair, stuck an arm akimbo, and smirked extravagantly by, wriggling his elbows and body, and drawling to his attendants: "Don't know yah; don't know yah, 'pon my soul, don't know yah!"

In *Edwin Drood*, the bridge takes on a sinister air. Edwin crosses it after encountering the ragged old woman who, unbeknown to him, is his uncle Jasper's opium dealer: 'by the river, the woman's words are in the rising wind, in the angry sky, in the troubled water, in the flickering lights'.

The original stone bridge on which these scenes were set was demolished in 1856, to be replaced by two rail and a new road bridge.

The Norman keep of **Rochester Castle (C)** impressed the Pickwickians as they crossed the bridge towards it. Alfred Jingle sums it up: 'glorious pile – frowning walls – tottering arches – dark nooks – crumbling staircases'.

Dickens brilliantly evokes the castle in *One Man In A Dockyard*, written for his magazine *Household Words* in 1851:

'I surveyed the massive ruin from the bridge and thought what a brief little practical joke I seemed to be, in comparison with its solidity, stature, strength, and length of life... I climbed the rugged staircase, stopping now and then to peep at great holes where the rafters and floors were once – bare as toothless gums now – or to enjoy glimpses of the Medway through dreary apertures like sockets without eyes.'

Next we reach **College Gate (D),** which bears a plaque stating it is Jasper's Gatehouse in *Edwin Drood*. While its location clearly fits that in the book, it is not big enough to contain the accommodation of John Jasper. William Hughes, in his 1891 guide *A Week's Tramp in Dickens-Land*, argues that the interior is actually based on **Deanery Gate (E),** which we find tucked down a path alongside the cathedral.

Hughes writes that this is: 'a quaint and very cosy old house, having ten rooms, some of which, together with the staircase, are beautifully panelled... this is the only one suitable for the residence of a person in Jasper's position'. As is often the case, Dickens has taken inspiration from more than one building and merged them to suit his purpose.

Deanery Gate, among the models for Jasper's Gatehouse in *The Mystery of Edwin Drood*

Close by is the side entrance to **Rochester Cathedral (F),** which Alfred Jingle sums up as: 'Old Cathedral too earthy smell – pilgrims' feet worn away the old steps – little Saxon doors – confessionals like money-takers' boxes at theatres – queer customers those monks – Popes, and Lord Treasurers, and all sorts of old fellows, with great red faces, and broken noses, turning up every day... – sarcophagus – fine place – old legends too – strange stories: capital.'

At the opening of *Edwin Drood* the cathedral is used in the revelation that John Jasper leads a double life. We have no sooner encountered him in a drug-induced stupor in a London opium den than he turns up here, rushing to don his robes and process into the cathedral with the choir he is master of. 'And then,' writes Dickens, 'the intoned words, "When the Wicked Man - " rise among groins of arches and beams of roof, awakening muttered thunder.'

The inscription on Dickens' plaque in the cathedral says it has been placed here: 'To connect his memory with the scenes in which his earliest and his latest years were passed and with the association of Rochester Cathedral and its neighbourhood which extended over all his life'.

Upon Dickens death, in 1870, plans were made – before a national campaign led to his burial in Westminster Abbey – to inter him in the little fenced-off

burial ground (G) between the cathedral and the castle. In *Edwin Drood* this spot is described as 'a fragment of a burial-ground in which an unhappy sheep was grazing'. Plans to bury him in the village of Shorne also had to be abandoned.

Minor Canon Row (H), which we come to next, is the Minor Canon Corner of *Edwin Drood*, where Neville Landless, who becomes prime suspect after the disappearance of Edwin, lodges with the Revd Septimus Crisparkle.

It is still instantly recognisable from Dickens' description in the novel: 'Red-brick walls harmoniously toned down in colour by time, strong-rooted ivy, latticed windows, panelled rooms, big oaken beams in

Rochester Castle, seen from Minor Canon Row

little places, and stone-walled gardens where annual fruit yet ripened upon monkish trees... a quiet place in the shadow of the Cathedral, which the cawing of the rooks, the echoing footsteps of rare passers, the sound of the Cathedral bell, or the roll of the Cathedral organ, seemed to render more quiet than absolute silence.'

As we walk up St Margaret's Street, we can pause to enjoy the view of the river from the churchyard of **St Peter with St Margaret (I)**. In *Edwin Drood*, it is at the riverside where Edwin is last seen, together with Neville Landless, sealing his guilt for many.

The river is dragged: 'All the livelong day the search went on; upon the river, with barge and pole, and drag and net; upon the muddy and rushy shore, with jack-boots, hatchet, spade, rope, dogs, and all imaginable appliances... but no trace of Edwin Drood revisited the light of the sun.'

Our next key location relates to Dickens' real life. It is the **birthplace of Ellen Lawless Ternan (J)**. Ellen – known as Nelly – was born on 3 March 1839 at 11 Upper Clarence Place, a terrace running north from what was then the King's Head pub and is now the Shonza restaurant, at 151 Maidstone Road. Her parents were actors who spent most of the year on tour, but for eight months around the time of her birth they rented a house here.

Dickens would not meet Nelly until 1857, when she was 18 and he was 45, and no longer in love with his wife. By that time, Ellen's father was dead, and her mother and sisters were struggling to make a living in the theatre. Dickens took them under his wing, seeking to further their careers, especially Nelly's.

As Claire Tomalin writes in *The Invisible Woman*, her biography of Nelly: 'As he asked her history, and she began to tell it, he made a discovery that can't have failed to stir him. Nelly… had been born in Rochester; and Rochester was the city where his own imagination had begun to flower. In Rochester he had first seen Shakespeare and pantomime; had written his own first play… Rochester was enshrined as the happy place of his own childhood. He had left it 15 years before Nelly appeared on the scene, but the coincidence was still extraordinary.'

He and Nelly embarked on a 13-year affair during which he abandoned his wife, and which only ended on his death. Nelly was to live another 40 years, and we will catch up with her once more in Margate, where she established a remarkable new life post-Dickens, in Walk 13.

The place where Dickens saw his first Shakespeare and pantomime was the Theatre Royal on Star Hill, now the **Conservative Club (K)**.

John Forster, in his *Life of Charles Dickens* writes: '"The sweet, dingy, shabby little country theatre" Charles Dickens was to call it, with the odour of sawdust, orange-peel and lamp-oil which he savoured all his life… the world here was transformed into farce and melodrama, and in all his accounts of his childhood expeditions to the theatre there can be sensed the unmistakeable hunger and intensity of Dickens' gaze… He loved the bad acting and the stage costumes, the absurdity of the actors and the banality of the plays, almost as if they were simulacra of life itself, and in all these accounts he conjures up the rapt vision of the child sitting in that "Dear, narrow, uncomfortable, faded-cushioned, flea-haunted, single tier of boxes" in the Theatre Royal.'

In *The Uncommercial Traveller* Dickens writes of this theatre, nostalgically: 'It was To Let, and hopelessly so… there had been no entertainment within its walls for a long time… It was mysteriously gone, like my own youth.'

Our next stop is at **The Vines (L)**, the old monks' vineyard, dating to before the Reformation. It features often in *Edwin Drood*. Here Edwin and Rosa sit on a bench beneath a cluster of elms, on the fateful night they decide to end their engagement. On Dickens' very last visit to Rochester – on Monday, 6 June, 1870, just three days before his death – he was noticed by several people leaning against the railings at The Vines. The final passage he wrote was set here: Dick Dachery, the mysterious figure who appears to be investigating Edwin Drood's disappearance, encounters the drug dealer Princess Puffer, who is on the trail of her client, John Jasper.

Restoration House, home to Miss Havisham in *Great Expectations*

Facing The Vines is **Restoration House (M)** Miss Havisham's home in *Great Expectations*, where it is called Satis House. It is here that Pip encounters – and is immediately in thrall to – the beautiful, imperious Estella. Upstairs, in the large music room that runs across the back of the house, is where Dickens places Miss Havisham's bedroom. The house is incredibly atmospheric, probably the best place in Rochester to get a sense of Dickens in a place he knew well. (See 'What you need to know' for details on arranging a visit')

Walking down to the High Street, **Eastgate House (N)** is the Nun's House of *Edwin Drood*, where Rosa and Helena Landless are schooled. In the park behind it, Dickens set the chilling scene in which, after Edwin Drood's disappearance, John Jasper corners Rosa and tells her he has loved her all along, but kept silent because she was engaged to Edwin, his nephew.

The Swiss Chalet which Dickens often wrote in at Gad's Hill Place stands in this park. (See Walk 1 for more on its significance.) The chalet presents a sorry sight today. Its rotting timbers are shored up with scaffolding poles, and a notice appeals for donations towards the £100,000 needed for its restoration.

The substantial Tudor building opposite Eastgate House has a role in both *Great Expectations* and *The Mystery of Edwin Drood* as, respectively **Mr Pumplechook's and Mr Sapsea's house (O)**.

Mr Pumblechook is the 'large hard-breathing middle-aged slow man' who introduces Pip to Miss Havisham, and who later claims to have been his first mentor.

In *Edwin Drood* it is the home of auctioneer and mayor Thomas Sapsea, 'the purest jackass in Cloisterham'. Dickens writes: 'Over the doorway is a wooden effigy, about half life-size, representing Mr Sapsea's father, in a curly wig and toga, in the act of selling.'

Dickens' Swiss chalet, where he wrote, now sadly in need of restoration

Our final point of interest is the aptly named **Six Poor Travellers' (P)** an almshouse where six penniless itinerants could be put up each night. It features in *The Seven Poor Travellers*, one of Dickens' Christmas tales, in which he imagines himself joining them on Christmas Eve.

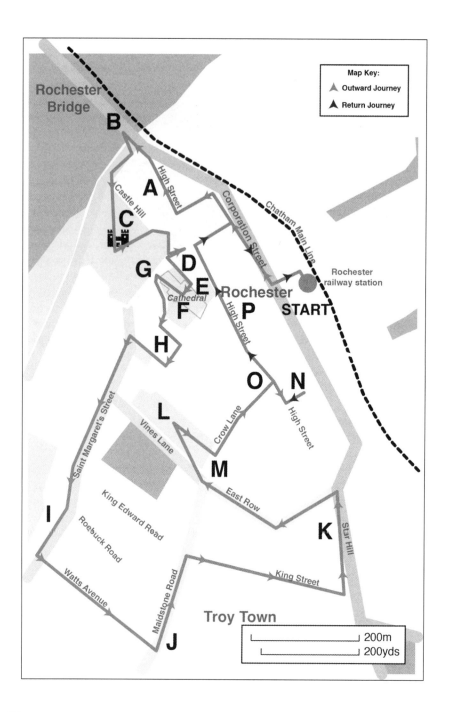

Map Key:
▲ Outward Journey
▲ Return Journey

Rochester Bridge

B

High Street

A

Castle Hill

C

Corporation Street

Chatham Main Line

G

D

E

Cathedral

F

Rochester

P

START

Rochester railway station

H

High Street

O

N

High Street

L

Crow Lane

Vines Lane

M

Saint Margaret's Street

King Edward Road

East Row

K

Star Hill

I

Roebuck Road

Watts Avenue

Maidstone Road

King Street

J

Troy Town

200m
200yds

THE WALK

What you need to know	
Distance	4.2km/2.6miles
Time	1 hour (not including stops)
Terrain	City pavements
Map	OS Explorer 163 Gravesend & Rochester OS Explorer 148 Maidstone & the Medway Towns
Starting point	Rochester railway station
How to get there	Car, parking off Corporation Street, or train
Key points along the way	Rochester Castle (C on the map) www.english-heritage.org.uk/visit/places/rochester-castle/ Rochester Cathedral (F) www.rochestercathedral.org Restoration House (M) www.restorationhouse.co.uk Eastgate house (O) www.visitmedway.org The Six Poor Travellers (P) www.richardwatts.org.uk/poor-travellers
Refreshments and accommodation	There are numerous good pubs, restaurants and hotels in Rochester. Sadly, at the time of writing, the Royal Victoria and Bull Hotel is awaiting refurbishment and cannot be recommended

Step-by-step directions

From Rochester railway station turn right and walk along Corporation Street for 200m/220yds, then turn left into George Lane. Turn right when you reach the High Street.

In 20m/22yds The Royal Victoria and Bull Hotel (A) will be on your left.

Pass the hotel and walk on to Rochester Bridge (B).

From Rochester Bridge retrace your steps to the Esplanade, turn right, cross the road and go up the step into the castle grounds (C).

From the castle, walk diagonally right through the grounds and leave via Boley Hill.

Turn right, and College Gate (D) is 30m/33yds ahead, on the High Street.

Turn around and walk back up Boley Hill.

Turn right just before the cathedral and walk up to Deanery Gate (E).

Turn around and you'll find a side door to Rochester Cathedral (F).

Leave the Cathedral by the main doorway, and the Old Burial Ground (G) among the places where Dickens wanted to be buried, is in front of you.

Turn left into College Yard and left again into Minor Canon Row (H).

Turn right and right again into The Precinct. At the end turn left into St Margaret's Street.

Walk 400m/440yds up St Margaret's Street to the Church of St Peter with St Margaret (I).

Continue up St Margaret's Street for 50m/55yds.

Turn left into Watts Avenue.

At the end of Watts Avenue, turn left into Maidstone Road.

Cross to the other side. Ellen Ternan's birthplace (J) is one of a terrace just past the Indian restaurant on the corner.

Continue down Maidstone Road for 200m/220yds to King Street.

Turn right into King Street.

After 300m/330yds, turn left into Delce Road.

At the end of Delce Road, bear left into Star Hill. The former Theatre Royal, now the Conservative club (K), is a few doors down, on your left.

Continue down Star Hill for a few metres to Victoria Street.

Turn left into Victoria Street then, in 100m/110yds, right into East Row.

In 100m/110yds turn right into Crow Lane for The Vines (L) and Restoration House (M).

Continue down Crow Lane for 100m/110yds to the High Street. Cross diagonally right for Eastgate House (N), and Dickens' chalet in the park beyond it.

Return to the High Street, where Mr Pumplechook's and Mr Sapsea's house (O) is opposite Eastgate House.

Continue along High Street for 200m/220yds for the Six Poor Travellers' house (P).

Continue along the High Street for 100m/110yds to Northgate.

Turn right into Northgate.

At the end of Northgate, turn right into Corporation Road.

Rochester railway station, our starting point, is 150m/165yds on the other side of the road.

WALK 5: A LOST
CHILDHOOD PLAYGROUND
CHATHAM TOWN TRAIL

One of Dickens' most nostalgic walks was through Chatham, taking in Fort Pitt, to the east of town, and then dipping down to the town centre before climbing west, up to Chatham Dockyard, before returning via The Lines and the River Medway.

This walk took in the key places from the formative years, aged four to 11, before Dickens' family moved to London.

As Peter Ackroyd says in his biography, *Dickens*: 'It is here, in what was sometimes called "the wickedest place in the world"... that we first begin to see Charles Dickens in situ; that we first begin to connect his infancy with his maturity, his childish imagination with his later fiction.

So let's catch up with the infant Charles at **Chatham Railway station (A)**, the scene of his lost childhood playground. When he moved here, this was a field, just in front of his house, where he used to play with his sister Fanny and his nurse, Mary Weller.

In *The Uncommercial Traveller*, Dickens described the shock of returning in 1860, over 40 years after his departure, to find his childhood idyll destroyed: 'It was gone. The two beautiful hawthorn trees, the hedge, the turf, and all those buttercups and daisies, had given place to the stoniest of jolting roads; while beyond the station, an ugly dark monster of a tunnel kept its jaws open, as if it had swallowed them and were ravenous for more destruction.'

Dickens remembered the flights of childhood fancy he had conjured up here: 'I looked in again over the low wall, at the scene of departed glories. Here, in the haymaking time, had I been delivered from the dungeons of Seringapatam, an immense pile (of haycock), by my own countrymen, the victorious British (boy next door and his two cousins), and had been recognised with ecstasy by my affianced one (Miss Green), who had come all the way from England (second house in the terrace) to ransom me, and marry me.'

In real life, Miss Green was Lucy Stroughill, who became Golden Lucy with 'a quantity of shining fair hair, clustering in curls all about her face' in the Christmas story, *The Wreck of the Golden Mary*. Lucy's brother, George, is said to have had some of the characteristics of the caddish Steerforth in *David Copperfield*.

The home that overlooked this field was **11 Ordnance Terrace (B)**, a flat-front, grey-brick place, numbered No 2 in Dickens' time. His parents John and Elizabeth had moved from Portsea to Chatham in 1816 or 17, John working in the naval pay office at Chatham Dockyard. They stayed in Chatham seven years: easily the happiest period in Dickens' childhood.

'Here it was,' says John Forster, Dickens friend and biographer, 'that his first desire for knowledge, and his greatest passion for reading, were awakened by his mother... she taught him regularly every day for a long time.'

Dickens' childhood home,
11 Ordnance Terrace

It is clear from his writings that Dickens remembered the house, and neighbours including George and Lucy, in great detail. Several other neighbours inspired characters in his early *Sketches by Boz*, published in various newspapers and periodicals between 1833 and 1836. Among them were a retired seaman who inspired the Half-pay Captain, 'a regular Robinson Crusoe' and the Old Lady, Miss Newnham at No 5, who was very kind to the Dickens children and would later leave money to the family.

From the window of Charles's attic bedroom he would have looked across Chatham to the tall-masted sailing ships on the river, the Dockyard and the Lines: a system of trenches, pits, passages and bomb-proof rooms where soldiers garrisoned in the town would engage in war games, and which would feature in a key scene of *The Pickwick Papers*.

This was a genteel neighbourhood. In his 1891 guide, *A Week's Tramp in Dickens-land*, William Hughes was invited in by the then owner, Mr Roberts. Hughes said the house 'has the dining room on the left-hand side, and the drawing-room on the first floor, and is altogether a pleasantly-situated, comfortable, and respectable dwelling.'

Dickens' profound love of family, friendship, conviviality and shared entertainment was born here. Mary Weller, who gave her surname to Sam Weller in *The Pickwick Papers*, and may have inspired Peggotty in *David Copperfield*, remembered how: 'Sometimes Charles would come downstairs and say to me, 'Now, Mary, clear the kitchen, we are going to have such a game … they would sing, recite, and perform parts of plays'. George Stroughill would sometimes bring in his Magic Lantern, an early type of photo projector.

In the visit described in *The Uncommercial Traveller*, Dickens turns from contemplating his old home: 'I left the place with a heavy heart for a walk all over the town,' and we shall follow him.

From the brow of **Fort Pitt (C)**, at the top of Ordnance Street, you can see the settings for scenes from *Great Expectations, David Copp*erfield and *The Pickwick Papers*. Indeed, we are standing on the spot where the duel in *The Pickwick Papers* took place. After a case of mistaken identity, the Pickwickian Winkle is almost forced to engage in mortal combat with Dr Slammer.

Slammer has mistaken Winkle for the decidedly slippery Alfred Jingle, who was wearing his distinctive Pickwick Society uniform at a ball in the Bull Hotel, Rochester and cut in on a lady the doctor was dancing with. Fortunately, Slammer realises the mistake in the nick of time, and Winkle's life is saved.

Walking down into the town, we reach a stretch of the **High Street (D)** around Ship Lane, Ship Pier and the Ship Inn which was a notorious place, avoided at night by everyone but drunken sailors. As Peter Ackroyd writes, Chatham when the Dickenses arrived, 'was a rough and dirty place, the haunt

The view over Chatham from Fort Pitt, alongside Dickens' childhood home

of sailors and soldiers. The Napoleonic Wars had just come to an end [in 1815]. This was now 'a place known for being "as lawless as it is squalid" and one in which the numerous frowsy drinking places were matched only by the number of equally frowsy brothels. We can be sure that the young Dickens noticed all of this; how much he understood is another matter. But, at a time before the moral restraint of what we have come to call the Victorian period, the less salubrious sights and odours were simply taken for granted.'

As an adult, Dickens did something about it. He supported the Chatham Mechanic's Institute, founded in 1837 to counter all the above through access to learning and culture and 'the promotion of useful knowledge among the working classes', and which had premises in this western end of the High Street.

William Hughes learns on his visit that: 'Charles Dickens was better known [in Chatham] in his latter years for his efforts, by readings and otherwise, to place the Mechanics' Institute on a sound basis and free from debt.' He was its president until his death in 1870, and gave readings there during the 1860s, raising £400.

As we progress down the High Street we reach **Military Road (E)**, where David Copperfield, 34 miles into his exhausting trek from London to Dover, penniless and having slept in the open on the Lines, has to sell his jacket to buy food.

He does so at a squalid little shop Dickens knew well, run by Old Charley, a notorious character. He writes: 'Into this shop, which was low and small, and which was darkened rather than lighted by a little window, overhung with clothes, and was descended into by some steps, I went with a palpitating heart; which was not relieved when an ugly old man, with the lower part of his face all covered with a stubbly grey beard, rushed out of a dirty den behind it, and seized me by the hair of my head.'

David is bullied into parting with the jacket for a mere four pence: 'I was so faint and weary that I closed with this offer; and taking the money out of his claw, not without trembling, went away more hungry and thirsty than I had ever been, a little before sunset.'

Where the jeweller H Samuel now stands on the corner of High Street and Military Road was, in Dickens' day, the Red Lion. William Hughes is told that William Budden, a pot-boy here, was the inspiration of the somnambulant fat boy in *Pickwick Papers*.

A few doors along, Where Primark is now at 198 High Street, stood the **Mitre Hotel and Clarence Inn (F)**, where Dickens gave his first public performance, aged eight or nine.

The landlord was John Tribe, who knew the Dickens family well. Charles and Fanny Dickens would be stood on a table to sing a then-popular duet, in which Charles took the part of a sailor wooing his sweetheart, singing 'Long time I've courted you, Miss' and Fanny replying 'I ne'er will wed a tar, Sir,' and with a chorus 'Sing toodledy, toodledy, bow wow wow.'

In 1821 Charles Dickens was sent to school at Mr Giles's Academy, tucked just behind the site of the inn in **Clover Street (G)** (then Clover Lane). The school was run by William Giles, and Dickens retained vivid memories of reciting verses from *The Humourist's Miscellany* in his first school examination, and receiving a double encore.

When the first few instalments of *Pickwick* had been published, William Giles sent its author a silver snuffbox, inscribed 'To the inimitable Boz'.

At the same time he joined the school, Dickens' father John began the slide into debt that would lead eventually to debtor's prison in London. The family was forced to move to **18 St Mary's Place (H)** a row of much meaner houses than Ordnance Terrace, which stood on The Brook, a site now buried beneath the Pentagon shopping centre.

Dickens was far less happy here. Mary Weller said: 'there were no such juvenile entertainments at this house as I had seen at the Terrace', but he found solace in reading. He used this experience in *David Copperfield,* writing: 'My father had left a small collection of books in a little room up-stairs, to which I had access (for it adjoined my own), and which nobody else in our house ever troubled. From that blessed little room... Tom Jones, Don Quixote... Robinson Crusoe came out, a glorious host to keep me company. They kept alive my fancy, and my hope of something beyond that place and time.'

Dickens recalled the eerie view at night from that upstairs window, of the graveyard at **St Mary's (I)**, in the painfully sad story *A Child's Dream of a Star*, which was inspired by his sadness over his sister Harriet, who died in childhood. In the tale, two children watch each night for 'one clear shining star that used to come out in the sky before the rest, near the church-spire, above the graves'.

But the little girl becomes ill, and dies: 'And so the time came, all too

St Mary's, the graveyard of which brought back painful memories of Dickens' dead sister

soon! when the child [Charles himself] looked out alone... and when there was a little grave among the graves, not there before; and when the star made long rays down towards him, as he saw it through his tears.'

Another memory of that house was of the tiles in the fireplace which carried scenes from the Scriptures, and which Dickens gave to Scrooge in *A Christmas Carol.*

Three of Charles' siblings were christened at this church, and in 1821 his aunt Mary was married here. Her groom was Dr Mathew Lambert, who inspired the irate Dr Slammer in *Pickwick.*

Up the hill beyond St Mary's is **Chatham Dockyard (J)** where Dickens' father worked as a pay clerk, and which the young Charles visited regularly. Here Dickens first heard the chant Old Clem, about St Clement, patron saint of blacksmiths, which he gives to Joe Gargery in *Great Expectations.*

The Dockyard features in *The Uncommercial Traveller*, where we read: 'It resounded with the noise of hammers beating upon iron; and the great sheds or slips under which the mighty men-of-war are built, loomed business-like... its great chimneys smoking with a quiet – almost a lazy – air, like giants smoking tobacco'.

Rising above Chatham on the dockyard side of town are **The Great Lines (K)**, a network of open spaces where, during the Napoleonic wars, troops would practice battle tactics, sometimes in hugely popular displays put on for the public. In *The Pickwick Papers* the Pickwickians get caught between two lines of advancing troops in one of these mock battles: 'There was a moment of intense bewilderment, a heavy tramp of footsteps, a violent concussion, a smothered laugh; the half-dozen regiments were half a thousand yards off, and the soles of Mr. Pickwick's boots were elevated in air.'

David Copperfield slept out in the open on the Lines because he was penniless: 'I sought no shelter, therefore but the sky; and toiling knot Chatham – which, in that night's aspect, is a mere dream of chalk and draw-bridges, and mastless ships in a muddy river, roofed like Noah's arks, – crept, at last, upon a sort of grass-grown battery overhanging a lane, where a sentry was walking too and fro. Here... I lay down near a cannon; and, happy in the society of the sentry's footsteps... slept soundly until morning.'

Dickens could see the **River Medway (L)** from St Mary's Place, as he had from Ordnance Terrace. Occasionally, Charles and Fanny would accompany their father on the Naval yacht, *Chatham*, on trips downriver to another dockyard, at Sheerness. On such trips he would have passed the prison hulks Euryalis and Canada, and the hospital ship Hercules, which inspired the story of the escaped convict Magwitch in *Great Expectations.*

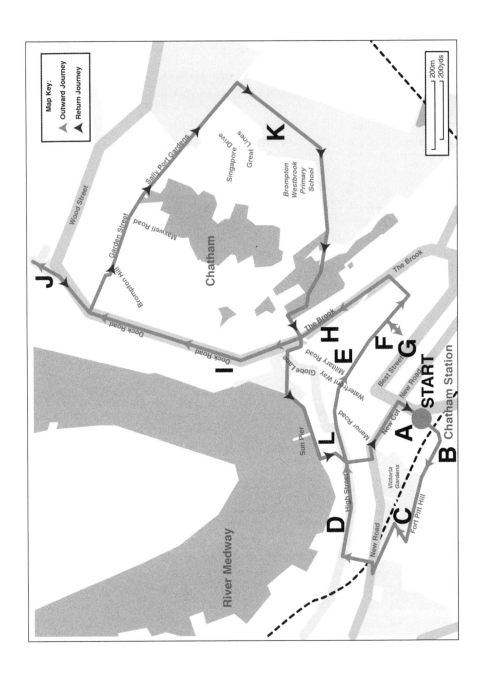

52

THE WALK

What you need to know	
Distance	6.87 km/4.9miles
Time	2.5 hours (not including stops)
Terrain	Pavements, with a steep descent from Fort Pitt, a sustained climb up to The Lines, followed by a sharp descent
Map	OS Explorer 163 Gravesend & Rochester OS Explorer 148 Maidstone & the Medway Towns
Starting point	Chatham railway station
How to get there	Train, or car
Key points along the way	Chatham Historic Dockyard www.thedockyard.co.uk
Refreshments and accommodation	Adjacent Rochester has more to offer, but these are on today's walk: St George Hotel (drink, food, accommodation) www.george-hotel.co.uk 01634 841012 The Canon, Garden Street (drink, food) www.thecannonpub.co.uk 01634 841006 The Command house, Dock Road (drink, food) 1634 921543

Step by step directions

From Chatham station (A) turn left and then almost immediately right into Ordnance Terrace and Dickens' former home at No. 11 (B).

Walk up Ordnance Terrace, which becomes Fort Pit Hill after 50m/55yds. In 100m/110yds at Fort Pitt (C) turn right and then immediately left, following the unmade road down to New Road.

Cross over and take the footpath to the left of the disused St Bartholomew's Hospital, leading to High Street.

Turn right into High Street. The area including Ship Lane and the site of the Mechanics' Institute (D) is on your left after 50m/55yds.

High Street crosses Military Road after 500m/550yds (E). The shop where David Copperfield sold his jacket for a pittance was here.

The Mitre Inn stood on the corner where Primark (F) is now.

Turn right into Clover Street after a few metres. Charles Dickens' school was here (G).

Retrace your steps to the High Street and turn right along it, then left into Batchelor Street, which leads to The Brook. Dickens' second home, in St Mary's Place, was on the left at the far end of the Pentagon Centre (H).

Follow the Brook for 400m/440yds and continue straight ahead up Dock Road to St Mary's Church (I).

After a further 400m/440yds you reach a footpath on the right signposted Saxon Shore Way. If you are visiting Chatham Dockyard (J), ignore this turning and continue straight on for 800m/880yds to the entrance. If not, cross the road and follow the signposted path, which leads to Garden Street. After 850m/930yds, when the road has become a footpath, turn right onto the Great Lines (K) and walk towards the towering naval war memorial. Follow the path to the left of it, which leads back down into Chatham after 350m/380yds.

Cross The Brook and turn almost immediately left into Globe Lane. Cross over and head for the path along the river (L).

Follow this path for 500m/550yds until it turns left and meets High Street. Turn right into High Street and then left into Hammond Hill.

At the end of Hammond Hill turn left into New Road, cross over and in 100m/110yds take New Cut and then turn right into Railway Street, which leads after 80m/88yds to Chatham Station.

Walk 6: Great Expectations Country 1
Lower Higham, Gravesend and Chalk circuit

This is a wonderful walk for experiencing the marshlands between Dickens' home at Higham and the Thames, the great river that flowed through his life and his fiction.

The walk, which for a long stretch follows the river bank, takes in Dickens' honeymoon cottage, and the model for Joe Gargery's forge in *Great Expectations*. It also passes the Thames-side pub where, in that novel, Pip and Magwitch are captured by the police, and a church he loved.

Gravesend is a frequent place of arrival and departure in Dickens' fiction. In *David Copperfield*, Mr Peggoty and Ham sail from here when they emigrate with Mr Micawber and his family to Australia. In *Bleak House*, it is one of the resorts where, during the summer, 'young clerks pine for bliss'.

The stretch of Thames downriver of Gravesend is broad and solitary, and Dickens used it in *Great Expectations* as the setting for Pip's attempt to smuggle Magwitch out of the country. Pip has learned that Magwitch, the terrifying figure he first encountered in a marsh churchyard, is the mystery benefactor who funded his education, and life as a young gentleman.

As a transportee for life, Magwitch has risked death by returning to observe how Pip, the boy he determined should have every advantage, has turned out. Now the police are on his tail as Pip sails with him to this stretch, Gravesend

The loneliness of Shorne Marshes

Reach, where he hopes to transfer his benefactor onto a ship bound for Hamburg or Antwerp, and safety.

It is still very possible today to recognise Dickens' description of how, in this quiet stretch of river, barges 'shaped like a child's first rude imitation of a boat, lay low in mud; and a little squat shoal lighthouse on open piles stood crippled in the mud on stilts and crutches; and slimy stakes stuck out of the mud, and slimy stones stuck out of the mud, and red land-marks and tide-marks stuck out of the mud, and an old landing-stage and an old roofless building slipped into the mud, and all about us was stagnation and mud.'

Pip has sought out a place 'where the water-side inhabitants are very few, and where lone public-houses are scattered here and there, of which we could choose one for a resting-place. There, we meant to lie by all night.'

They chose The Ship, a pub modelled on **The Ship and Lobster (A)**, which today stands among the wharves and warehouses on the eastern edge of Gravesend. The pub, sadly recently closed at the time of writing, was a regular stopping point for Dickens on his walks to Gravesend.

In *Great Expectations* we read: 'It was a dirty place enough, and I daresay not unknown to smuggling adventures; but there was a good fire in the

The Thames at Gravesend Reach

kitchen, and there were also eggs and bacon to eat, and various liquors to drink... I lay down with the greater part of my clothes on, and slept well for a few hours. When I awoke, the wind had risen, and the sign of the house (The Ship) was creaking and banging about, with noises that startled me.' Shortly afterwards, the police pounce.

The area around Gravesend's **Town Pier (B)** is a good place to stop for lunch, before retracing our steps to the edge of town, where we pick up a path alongside the Thames and Medway Canal, dug in 1825 to enable ships to travel to and from Chatham and Rochester, avoiding a long river voyage of 47 miles. It was only fully operational for 20 years, before its route was stopped when the railway took over its tunnel between Lower Higham and Strood.

Leaving the canal to tack across the fields, we come to the village of Chalk, home to three significant Dickens locations. The first is his honeymoon home, **Craddock's Cottage (C)**. which has a bust of Dickens and an inscription above the door.

While here, in April 1836, Dickens wrote the second instalment of *The Pickwick Papers* – chapters three to five. Claire Tomalin, in *Charles Dickens: A life*, says 'Dickens wanted to show [his new wife] Catherine the country of his childhood and no

Dickens' honeymoon cottage, in Chalk

doubt hoped to walk with her to favourite spots... in the April sunshine.' Sadly, however, 'Catherine was never a great walker.'

The couple's first son, Charley, was born exactly nine months after their stay here. They returned for two months in 1838, while Dickens was writing *Oliver Twist*. At the time, Catherine was suffering from post-natal depression, and they came partly for her health.

William Hughes, in his 1891 guide, *A Week's Tramp in Dickens-Land*, spoke to a local who told him how he often encountered the author striding through the village, and of how: 'the brisk walk of Charles Dickens was always slackened, and he never failed to glance meditatively for a few moments at the windows of [Craddock's Cottage] a corner house advantageously situated for commanding views of the river and the far-stretching landscape beyond.'

A little way up the road is another significant location: the model for **Joe Gargery's Forge (D)** in *Great Expectations*. This is an example of Dickens taking a building which suited his purposes but transporting it to another location: in this case to Pip's village, which is actually based on Lower Higham, and which we explore in Walk 7.

The forge and adjoining weatherboard cottage were, at the time, exactly as described in *Great Expectations*, and are still instantly recognisable today. Pip says of it: 'Joe's forge adjoined our house, which was a wooden house, as many of the dwellings in our country were – most of them, at that time.'

A door led straight from the forge into the kitchen, where Joe would often be found, sitting in his chair at the corner of the large open fireplace. The last blacksmith left in 1953 but, in his 1929 book *Great Expectations Country*, William Gadd learned: 'Mr Mullender, the present blacksmith, tells me that his grandmother, who resided in the village from 1828 until her death in 1909, used to tell him about a morose and disagreeable journeyman they had at the forge during her early years there.' This man fits the description of Dolge Orlick, the violent misanthrope who seems likely to have attacked Joe's wife Georgiana, Pip's sister.

Some critics believe *Great Expectations* demonstrates a mournful sense of lost innocence, and see as significant the fact that the period this novel was forming in Dickens' mind coincided with his rejection, in 1858, of his wife.

The model for Joe Gargery's Forge, in Chalk

Yet here Dickens is, walking regularly past their honeymoon home, and basing Joe's forge on a house nearby. Paul Schlicke, in *The Oxford Reader's Companion to Dickens,* comments: 'There can have been fewer places for Dickens more likely to call up a sense of lost innocence than Chalk.'

Our final point of interest is the 11th century church of **St Mary (E)** a mile from the village and just off the A226 which, in Dickens' day, would have given a direct but quiet route back to Gad's Hill. This was another place he liked to pause.

William Hughes describes a now very worn stone figure carved above the church's doorway: 'This figure represents an old priest in a stooping position, with an upturned vessel (probably a jug)... Dickens used to be a great admirer of this quaint carving, and it is said that whenever he passed it, he always took off his hat to it, or gave it a friendly nod, as to an old acquaintance.'

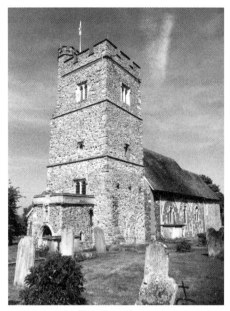

St Mary's, Chalk, a favourite stopping point for Dickens

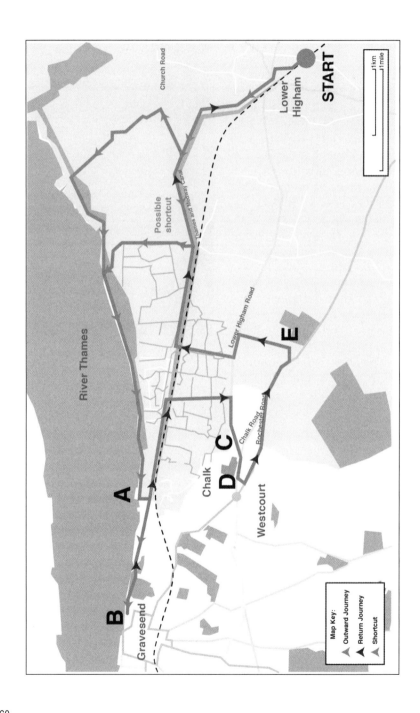

THE WALK

What you need to know	
Distance	Full route: 25.1km/15.6miles Shortened route: 21.1km/13.1miles
Time	Full route: 5 hours 30 minutes (not including stops) Shortened route:
Terrain	Mainly flat grassland, some pavement walking
Map	OS Explorer 163 Gravesend & Rochester
Starting point	Higham railway station
How to get there	Train, or car, parking at railway station or in village
Refreshments and accommodation	Gravesend offers a range of facilities. The following are on our walk: The Three Daws (drink, food) Town Pier, Gravesend. www.threedaws.co.uk 01474 566869 Clarendon Royal Hotel (drink, food, accommodation) Royal Pier Rd, Gravesend. www.clarendonroyalhotel.co.uk 01474 362221

Step-by-step directions

Turn right out of Higham station, joining School Lane, cross the railway bridge, and walk for 100m/110yds to Canal Road.

Turn left into Canal Road.

Continue for 1.6km/1mile until you pass under a railway bridge.

Routes here diverge. To continue on the long route, read on. For an alternative route, drop down to 'Possible shortcut' below.

Turn right onto the footpath immediately after the bridge.

Follow the footpath alongside the railway track for 600m/660yds.

At a T-junction, where the path to the right goes over the railway tracks, turn left, and follow the track across the marshes for 1.5km/.9miles until you reach the Thames.

Turn left and follow the river upstream for 4km/2.5miles to the outskirts of Gravesend. This section of the route is on the Saxon Shore Way, so you can follow signs for it.

Turn left opposite a long jetty, after the now closed Ship and Lobster pub. (A) After 100m/110yds, turn right onto a track signposted Saxon Shore Way which passes between old wharves and warehouses.

After 600m/660yds you will reach the canal basin marina. Continue for 800m/880yds, following signs for the Saxon Shore Way until you reach the Town Pier. (B)

This is a good point for a break.

Now retrace your steps for 1.8km/1.1miles, following the Saxon Shore Way signs, until you reach the long-disused Thames and Medway Canal. Follow the canal-side path for 1.4km/.86miles until a path on your right crosses the canal and railway. Caution: take care crossing the tracks, there are two sets of rails.

Follow this path between hedges for 600m/660yds until it reaches Lower Higham Road.

Turn right and follow Lower Higham Road for 1.1km/.7miles.

Just before the junction with Chalk Road you will see the back of a white weatherboarded house on your left. This house, a couple of doors down Chalk Road, is where Dickens spent his honeymoon (C).

From the house, revert to your previous direction, heading west along Lower Higham Road for 400m/440yds.

Turn left into Forge Lane. The house on the corner is the model for Joe Gargery's forge in Great Expectations. (D)

Continue up Forge Lane for 80m/88yds until you reach the Gravesend Road, A226.

Turn left and follow Gravesend Road for 1.4km/.86miles until you reach Church Lane.

Turn left into Church Lane.

After 200m/220yds you will reach St Mary's Church (E).

Continue down Church Lane for 800m/880yds until it reaches the Lower Higham Road.

Turn left. After 200m/220yds, take the track on your right that leads over fields, and crosses the railway and canal after 800m/880yds.

Turn right and follow the canal-side footpath for 3.7km/2.3miles back to Lower Higham.

Turn right at the crossroads at the end of Canal Road to return to Higham station.

Possible shortcut

To cut approximately 4km/2.5miles from your walk, there is a more direct route over the marshes, but it crosses a Metropolitan Police firing range, and the route can be closed without notice during practice sessions. When it is closed, red flags fly and you will be turned back.

It is not possible to find out in advance whether this path will be closed.

If you want to risk it, continue straight on – instead of turning right – after the railway bridge, and follow the canal side path for 1.4km/.86miles until a track leads off to the right.

Follow it across Shorne Marshes until you reach the river after 1km/.62miles. Turn left and pick up the main route described above.

WALK 7: GREAT EXPECTATIONS COUNTRY 2
LOWER HIGHAM, EGYPT BAY AND COOLING CIRCUIT

In *Great Expectations* the landscape we cover on this walk is described as: 'A most beastly place. Mudbank, mist, swamp... swamp, mist, and mudbank.' Do not be put off! In fact, this is an incredibly atmospheric place, and wonderful walking country.

As William Gadd wrote in *The Great Expectations Country*, his 1929 exploration of the places in the novel, this has always been a neglected part of Kent. 'Yet,' he writes, 'this piece of country has a charm and interest peculiar to itself, unlike any other part of Kent. Perhaps it is the ever-present marshes

Lower Higham church, where Pip met Magwitch and Dickens' daughter Katey was married

and the wide rivers bounding the prospect on either hand; the scarcity of human beings; the unchanged quaint little churches and taverns in the scattered villages and hamlets; or perhaps it is because the Spirit of Dickens and *Great Expectations* pervades the land.'

The spirit of Dickens the serious walker is definitely here. This route is one of the longest regular walks he took, at a hardcore 20.25miles. I promise you, it's worth it. But if you prefer a shorter route, which still takes in the key locations of *Great Expectations*, you'll find a 18.2km/ 11.3miles alternative route also outlined below.

Whichever option you take, there are some unexpected discoveries along the way.

The lonely marshes between Lower Higham and the Thames

It is commonly believed that Pip's village in the book is based on Cooling but, through his painstaking detective work, William Gadd makes a strong case for Dickens actually having had Lower Higham in mind, and merely importing other locations he liked, including Joe Gargery's forge from Chalk, and the distinctive childrens' gravestones from Cooling, to this location.

When Gadd asked a local for his opinion on the Cooling/Lower Higham question, he replied: 'Is it supposed to be Cooling? Why, it is Lower Higham.' On the ground, it is clear the geography doesn't fit the general assumptions. In *Great Expectations*, Pip's village is 'a mile or more from the church... on the flat in-shore among the alder trees and pollards.' That describes Lower Higham exactly while, in Cooling, the church is in the centre of the village, and the village is surrounded by farmland, not on the edge of the marsh.

Not that it matters too much. As John Forster, Dickens friend and biographer points out, he took what he wanted from nature and reality, and rearranged the pieces to suit his literary purpose. In any case, we will take in all the places he used in the mix.

Shortly after we leave Higham railway station and are passing through Chequers Street, you will notice a former pub on the corner of Church Street and Canal Road. This, until a few years ago, was **The Chequers Inn (A)**, and it replaced an older Chequers which exactly fitted Dickens' description of the pub in *Great Expectations*: The Three Jolly Bargemen.

The Chequers' then landlord showed William Gadd a faded photo of the original tavern, demolished in 1900, and well known to Dickens. It was here, this evidence suggests, that Joe Gargery went to smoke his pipe, where the mysterious stranger gave Pip a shilling wrapped in two greasy one-pound notes and who pointedly stirred his drink with a file, and where, in the little bar parlour, Mr Jaggers came to tell Pip that an anonymous benefactor wanted to make him rich, and a gentleman.

Lower Higham was also, Gadd concludes, the location for the church on the marshes where, in one of the most striking scenes in English literature, Pip encounters the escaped convict Magwitch. That church is **St Mary the Virgin (B)**. Everything about it, and its location, fits the opening passage of the novel, in which we read:

'The man, after looking at me for a moment, turned me upside down, and emptied my pockets. There was nothing in them but a piece of bread. When the church came to itself – for he was so sudden and strong that he made it go head over heels before me, and I saw the steeple under my feet – when the church came to itself, I say, I was seated on a high tombstone, trembling while he ate the bread ravenously.'

As Gadd says: 'all the other churches in the peninsula... have square stone towers, but Lower Higham Church has a quaint timber steeple, shingled with tiles and looking like an old-fashioned candle extinguisher' and is the only one to fit the description in the novel.

The location fits too. St Mary's is a 'lonely' church, well away from the village is serves, unlike St James' in Cooling.

St Mary's was also the setting of a highly significant event in Dickens' family life. On July 17 1860, three months before he began writing *Great Expectations*, his daughter Katey was married here.

Ostensibly, this was a happy occasion. The villagers turned out en-masse to see Katey, in her bridal gown and with orange blossom in her auburn hair, as she drove with her father under triumphal arches to this little country church.

Yet Katey did not love the man she was marrying: the aesthetic, tight-fisted and probably impotent Charles Collins, brother of Dickens' friend, protege and collaborator Wilkie Collins. And, because of the bitterness of her parents' recent separation, Katey's mother Catherine was not present.

Dickens was unhappy about the match, convinced his daughter was marrying to get away from him and the unhappy home Gad's Hill Place had become since he rejected Catherine. He was right. For all these reasons, as

Paul Schlicke writes in *The Oxford Reader's Companion to Dickens*, St Mary's 'must have been a place imbued with anxiety for Dickens'.

That evening, Dickens' eldest daughter Mamie went up to her sister's bedroom. She found her father on his knees, his face pressed against Katey's wedding gown, sobbing uncontrollably.

In Dickens' day, before embankments were built alongside the Thames, the marsh came right up to the churchyard wall. Now, as we walk towards the river, we cross farmland to reach **Cliffe Fort (C)**. The fort stands where The Battery does in *Great Expectations*, and is the spot to which Magwitch ordered Pip to bring a file and 'wittles'.

The Battery was one of a number of such fortifications built in 1539 under Henry VIII to counter the threat of invasion from the French. It was replaced by the now ruined and fenced off Cliffe Fort in 1870, within 10 years of the publication of *Great Expectations*.

Cliffe Fort, site of the Battery, where Pip was forced to bring food for the convict Magwitch

This is also where Pip spends summer afternoons lounging on the grass banks with Joe, his brother-in-law and surrogate father, while he tries to teach him to read:

'The old Battery out on the marshes was our place of study, and a broken slate and a short piece of slate-pencil were our educational implements: to which Joe always added a pipe of tobacco. I never knew Joe to remember anything from one Sunday to another, or to acquire, under my tuition, any piece of information whatever. Yet he would smoke his pipe at the Battery with a far more sagacious air than anywhere else – even with a learned air – as if he considered himself to be advancing immensely.'

When Pip first encounters Magwitch, he and another prisoner have escaped from one of a number of prison hulks: condemned battleships with their rigging removed anchored along the Thames, to the east of the Battery, to house convicts. Magwitch had struggled for some miles through the mud of the marsh before he reaches the churchyard and encounters Pip.

The location of the hulk was **Egypt Bay (D)**, 5 miles east of the Battery. In Dickens' time, says William Gadd, the coastguard lookout vessel, *The Swallow*, was moored at this sandy natural harbour, to counter smuggling. Dickens used the spot, substituting a prison hulk for the coastguard ship he would have seen here on his walks. When Dickens was a boy, in Chatham, there were convict ships moored in the river. Gadd says: 'The prison ship Dickens described was one of three convict hulks that were moored in the Medway.'

Once we reach Cooling we have left the marshes far behind. The village pub, the **Horseshoe and Castle (E)** is the other candidate for The Three Jolly Bargemen in the novel, alongside The Chequers in Lower Higham. Whether it is or not, it has the distinct advantage over the Chequers of still being open. It is also conveniently close to **St James' (F)** churchyard and the 13 distinctive graves that inspired Dickens. They memorialise young children from two branches of the Comport family who died of malaria in the eighteenth century.

Dickens reduced the total to five in the novel, and has Pip imagine that the swaddled shape of these 'stone lozenges' indicated that his five little brothers 'had all been born on their backs with their hands in their trousers-pockets, and never taken them out in this state of existence'.

John Forster tells us that Dickens often brought friends here to show them the graves. James Fields, an American publisher, recalled a picnic in the graveyard. He wrote of how Dickens 'had chosen a good flat gravestone in one corner... had spread a wide napkin thereon after the fashion of a domestic dinner table, and was rapidly transferring the contents of the hamper to that point.

'The horrible whimsicality of trying to eat and make merry under these deplorable circumstances, the tragic-comic character of the scene, appeared to take him by surprise. He at once threw himself into it... with fantastic eagerness. Having spread the table after the most approved style, he suddenly disappeared behind the wall for a moment, transformed himself by the aid of a towel and napkin into a first-class head-waiter, reappeared, laid down a row of plates along the top of the wall, as at a bar-room or eating house, again retreated to the other side with some provisions, and, making the gentlemen stand up to the wall, went through the whole play with the most entire gravity.'

While they ate, two tramps watched them, and Dickens decided they too should have food and wine, but said to the women among the picnic party 'You shall carry it to them, it will be less like charity and more like a kindness if one of you should speak to the poor souls!'

The graves of child malaria victims at Cooling church which inspired Dickens

THE WALK

What you need to know	
Distance	Full route: 32.6km/20.25miles Shorter route: 18.2km/11.3miles
Time	Full route: 8 hours 20 minutes (not including stops) Shorter route: 3 hours 45 minutes (not including stops)
Terrain	Generally level grassland, some road walking, steady ascent up Northward Hill (on full route only), between Egypt Bay and Cooling
Map	OS Explorer 163 Gravesend & Rochester
Starting point	Higham railway station
How to get there	Train, or car to Higham, parking at railway station or in village
Key points along the way	St Mary's church, Lower Higham (B). Open daily 9am-6pm www.visitchurches.org.uk St James' church, Cooling (F). Open daily 10am-4pm www.visitchurches.org.uk
Refreshments and accommodation	The Horseshoe and Castle (E), Cooling (drink, food, accommodation) www.horseshoeandcastle.com 01634221691 Shorter route only: The Six Bells, Cliffe (drink, food, accommodation) www.sixbellscliffe.co.uk 01634 221459

Step-by-step directions

From Higham railway station turn left to cross the railway and walk north for 100m/110yds to reach Church Street. The now-closed Chequers pub is on the corner (A).

Take Church Street for 1.2km/.75miles to reach St Mary's church (B).

Continue north for 600m/660yds as the route becomes a track and crosses a

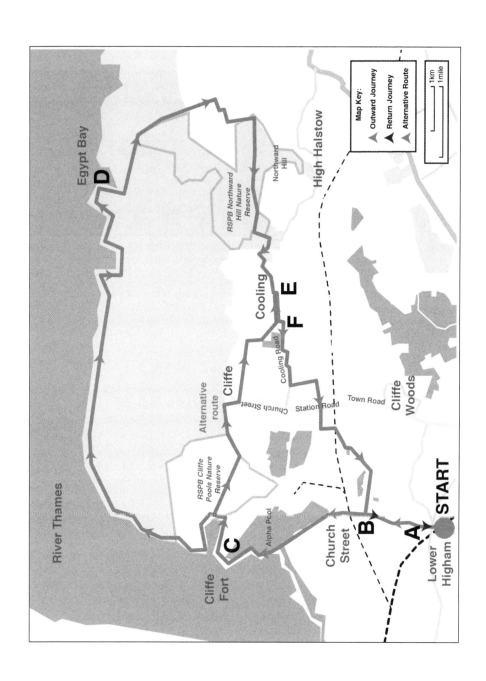

single-track railway.
When the path forks, take the left-hand route, keeping the lakes to your right.

Continue for 1km/.6miles, passing a narrow strip of land separating two lakes, until you reach the river bank.

Here we join the Saxon Shore Way path.

Note: at this point the way can become waterlogged. You may find you need to tack either left or right to skirt any standing water.

Continue straight ahead along the river bank for 1km/.6miles to the remains of Cliffe Fort, site of the Battery (C). Follow the signposted footpath through the gravel works and as it curves left around Cliffe Creek.

After 600m/660yds, at the end of the creek, our alternative routes divide.

Long route directions continue from here
(To take the short route, drop down to where you see 'Short route directions continue here')

Take the path that curves left along the other bank of the creek.

At the sea wall, follow the path round to the right.

After 7km/4.3miles you will be directed around a new harbour which, unless you have the latest map, may not be marked.

After 2.5km/1.5miles you rejoin the river bank and, in 100m/110yds, reach Egypt Bay (D).

After 500m/550yds, when you reach the inner point of the bay's western shore, follow the path for 750m/820yds as it cuts inland along the top of an old earth sea defence.

After passing to the north of Decoy Fleet, take the right-hand track when the way forks and join a farm track marked Manor Way on OS maps.

Follow Manor Way for 1.4km/.9miles until it becomes a tarmacked lane at Swigshole.

Follow the lane for 1.2km/.75miles as it switches right, then left, then right, then left again and begins to climb up Decoy Hill and a wood appears on your right.

200m/220yds after the wood begins, take the footpath on your right which climbs up through the trees for a further 200m/220yds.

When you emerge into a field, follow the path to the field margin on your right for 175m/190yds until you reach a path crossing yours at right angles.

Turn right here, on what is the Saxon Shore Way, which we now follow west for 300m/330yds until it reaches the RSPB reserve at Northward Hill.

Take care as you reach the woodland to follow the correct path. You want to head north west through the wood, avoiding the wide grassy path that runs just to the south of it. Saxon Shore Way signs are poor at this point.

After 800m/880yds you will emerge from the wood. Keep on the same path for 600m/660yds until you reach a farm track. Turn left.

After 250m/275yds, having passed Eastborough Farm, look for a track branching right to Bromhey Farm.

Follow this track for 400m/440yds, following the Saxon Shore Way signs that take you directly through the farmyard before taking a right-angled turn left.

After 300m/330yds, turn right when you reach a lane (Cooling Road) and follow it for 800m/880yds until you see the Horseshoe and Castle pub on your left (E).

St Luke's church is 600m/660yds past the pub, where the lane turns sharp left and then almost immediately right (F).

Short route directions continue here

Turn left at the end of the creek and then almost immediately take the path that turns right, running between two lakes for 750m/820yds.

Where paths go left and right, turn left and continue for 500m/550yds.

Continue for 500m/550yds along Pickles Way (ignoring the path that runs off to the left after 300m/330yds) to Cliffe village.

Follow the lane, which becomes Pond Hill and then Church Street, through the village, turning right after 250m/275yds into Swingate Avenue, and right again as Swingate Avenue continues, reaching the edge of the village after 400m/440yds.

Continue straight ahead for 900m/990yds as the route, marked Saxon Shore Way, leads across a field to Common Lane.

Turn right into Common Lane, then take the footpath that leaves the road on the left after 200m/220yds.

Follow the path as it skirts an orchard then crosses a field, leading after 500m/550yds to Cooling Road.

Turn right into Cooling Road to reach St James' church (F) and the Horseshoe and Castle pub (E).

After visiting the pub and/or church, retrace your steps along Cooling Road, and follow it for 1.7km/1.05mile.

At Morning Cross Cottages turn left, where a sign reads 'Byway Well Penn Road'.

After 500m/550yds take the dirt track on your right, which reaches Station Road after 550m/600yds.

Turn left into Station Road, then almost immediately right.

Continue for 350m/380yds and turn left at the T junction.

After 350m/380yds, take the footpath on the right immediately after the lane crosses over the railway tracks. The path runs diagonally right over the field towards a small wood. The path is usually clear, being reinstated after ploughing.

At the wood take the footbridge and follow the path south for 100m/110yds, crossing another footbridge to emerge in a field. Follow the usually clearly marked footpath for 500m/550yds until you reach a tarmacked farm track.

Turn right and follow the track for 750m/820yds until it meets Church Street.

Turn left into Church Street and follow it for 1.5km/.9miles back to Lower Higham, and our starting point at the railway station.

Walk 8: 'One of the most beautiful walks in England'
Rochester to Bluebell Hill, Sandling, Allington and Aylesford

Charles Dickens wrote, in 1857: 'I have discovered that the route between Rochester and Maidstone is one of the most beautiful walks in England.'

There may have been a certain nostalgia in the choice, for the places this walk took Dickens had featured prominently in his first novel, *The Pickwick Papers*, written over 20 years earlier in 1836.

Our route takes in the key points along the way, but stops short of the suburbs around Maidstone, ending instead at the picturesque village of Aylesford, from which we return to Rochester by train.

We climb from Rochester over Bluebell Hill, a favourite picnic spot for Dickens, and go on to explore the grounds of Cobtree Hall at Sandling – the models, in *The Pickwick Papers*, for Manor Farm and Dingley Dell respectively. We finish up in Aylesford, which has a disguised role in *Pickwick*.

The area also inspired later fiction. The weir in Dickens' last, unfinished novel *The Mystery of Edwin Drood* is based on Allington Lock, which we visit on our way to Aylesford.

Dickens loved the spectacular views from **Bluebell Hill (A)** across the Medway valley. In later life he was fond of bringing friends here for picnics. On such occasions they would ride over from his home at Gad's Hill Place, Higham, with a great hamper. In a letter to a friend, written in 1860, Dickens said: 'I wish I could carry you off to a favourite spot of mine between [Gad's Hill] and Maidstone... We often take our lunch on a hillside there in the summer, and then I lay down on the grass – a splendid example of laziness.'

In 1868 Dickens brought the American poet Henry Wadsworth Longfellow here. Longfellow was a *Pickwick* super-fan. As a young man he had been so taken with the adventures of the Pickwickians that he had formed a club, the Five of Clubs, with four friends, went on adventures in imitation of them, and spoke in Wellerisms: phrases in imitation of the off-beat Cockney wisdom of Sam Weller, Pickwick's servant. The poet and his daughter, Alice, came to Bluebell Hill on a Sunday afternoon drive through *Pickwick* country which Dickens said 'was like a holiday ride in England 50 years ago'.

In her journal, Alice Longfellow wrote: 'We drove... in a carriage and pair with a postillion in a red jacket instead of a coachman, in fine style and we

The view from Dickens' favourite picnic spot on Bluebell Hill

expected to meet all the *Pickwick* characters at every turn.' They ended up at 'some Druidical stones'.

Those stones were **Kit's Coty House (B)**, the remnants of a 6,000-year-old Stone Age burial chamber, which we encounter on our way down Bluebell Hill, just off the ancient green way that takes us, between thick yew hedges, into the valley.

Kit's Coty House

It may be that the episode where Pickwick finds an old sarsen stone in Cobham and wrongly concludes that a contemporary inscription on it is of ancient origin was inspired here. What looks at first like a cryptic message:

> +
> B I L S T
> U M
> P S H I
> S. M.
> A R K

turns out to read: 'Bill Stumps his mark'.

Charles Dickens came across **Cobtree Manor (C)**, and its then-owner, William Spong when, on a winter skating expedition, he fell through the ice on a pond close to the house, plunging into freezing water. He sought help at the manor and struck up a friendship with Spong. Dickens was to base the amiable Mr Wardle, who the Pickwickians meet on the Great Lines at Chatham, on Spong. Samuel Pickwick and friends accept an invitation to stay at Cobtree Manor – Manor Farm in the book – and it features in several key episodes.

We approach it from the north, experiencing the seclusion in which Dickens described the house as standing, entering grounds which are now a public park and passing a tree-fringed pond to the east of the house.

Dickens has the Pickwickians spend Christmas here, and echoes his mishap on the ice in an episode involving Samuel Pickwick, who is persuaded, having seen the effortless way in which Sam Weller and the Fat Boy perform masterly slides along the ice, to have a go himself:

'The sport was at its height, the sliding was at the quickest, the laughter was at the loudest, when a sharp smart crack was heard. There was a quick rush towards the bank, a wild scream from the ladies, and a shout from Mr Tupman. A large mass of ice disappeared; the water bubbled up over it; Mr Pickwick's hat, gloves, and handkerchief were floating on the surface; and this was all of Mr Pickwick that anybody could see.'

In the 1960s Cobtree Manor was owned by Sir Garrard Tyrwhitt-Drake, who ran the largest private zoo in Europe in the grounds, featuring lions, tigers and elephants. He left the estate in a trust to benefit the people of Maidstone. The house is privately owned, but the estate is now a public park, through which we walk.

Cobtree Manor is much changed, but what has become known as the Dickens Dining Room has survived and is still recognisable as 'the old parlour' described in *Pickwick*, with its grand inglenook fireplace, walls decorated with 'ancient samplers' and 'worsted landscapes' and the central beam on which can still be seen the letters A and B, denoting the fact that the boundary between the parishes of Boxley and Allington runs through the room.

Here the Pickwickians play games of whist, enjoy 'a substantial though homely supper' and declare: 'There ain't a better spot o' ground in all Kent, sir.'

At **Allington Lock (D)** we move from scenes in Dickens' first novel to a key one in his last, *The Mystery of Edwin Drood*. The Lock, which marks the point at which the Medway ceases to be tidal, is the likely model for Cloisterham Weir. This is the place where Edwin Drood and Neville Landless come after a bitter row. Edwin is never seen again after this outing, leading to suspicions that Neville has murdered him.

It is also the place where Septimus Crisparkle, minor canon at the cathedral, spots a vital clue: 'He threw off his clothes, he plunged into the icy water, and swam for the spot – a corner of the weir – where something glistened which did not move and come over with the glistening water drops, but remained stationary... He brought the watch to the bank, swam to the weir again, climbed it, and dived off... He dived and dived and dived, until he could bear the cold no more. His notion was that he would find the body; he only found a shirt-pin sticking in some mud and ooze.'

Allington Lock, scene of the crime in *The Mystery of Edwin Drood*

In the novel, the weir is said to be only two miles from Cloisterham (Rochester) but Dickens used poetic license to move it five miles or so upstream.

Aylesford, reached after a pleasant waterside walk from Allington, and where we end our walk, is a possible point at which the Pickwickians cross the river via the old **stone bridge (E)** on their way to Muggleton – West Malling

Aylesford's old bridge, where the Pickwickians may have crashed their carriage

77

– to watch a cricket match, as explored in Walk 9. Dickens' son Charley believed this was the spot his father had in mind, despite the ancient stone bridge becoming a wooden one in the novel.

It is here that the Pickwickians suffer a mishap with the carriage and pair they have rented when the lead horse is startled by a loud noise:

'He tore off with the four-wheeled chaise behind him... Mr Tupman threw himself into the hedge, Mr Snodgrass followed his example, the horse dashed the four-wheeled chaise against a wooden bridge, separated the wheels from the body... and finally stood stock still to gaze upon the ruin he had made.'

Aylesford churchyard holds the grave of William Spong, model for Mr Wardle, his stone recording that he died on November 15 1839.

THE WALK

What you need to know	
Distance	21km/13miles
Time	5 hours 45 minutes (not including stops)
Terrain	Mainly downland paths with one sustained ascent for first third of walk, followed by a sustained descent. Short stretches on pavements, and one on generally traffic-free lanes
Map	OS Explorer 148 Maidstone & The Medway Towns
Starting point	Rochester Bridge
How to get there	Train to Rochester, or car, parking in Corporation Street, Rochester. Note: return route by train, from Aylesford to Rochester
Refreshments and accommodation	Robin Hood (drink, food) 364 Common Road, Bluebell Hill. www.robinhood-pub.co.uk 01634 861500 Cobtree Manor Park Cafe (drink, food) www.cobtreecafe.co.uk 01622 239989 Malta Inn, Allington Lock (drink, food) 01622 717 251 The Chequers (drink, food) Aylesford http://thechequersaylesford.co.uk/ 01622 717286

Step by step directions

From the south end of Rochester Bridge, turn left, following The Esplanade along the river Medway for 2km/1.25miles.

When The Esplanade becomes Shorts Way and turns left, continue straight on along a footpath for 600m/660yds.

Turn left and follow the path up between back gardens for 500m/550yds until you reach Wouldham Road.

Turn right on Wouldham Road and follow it beneath the M2 motorway.

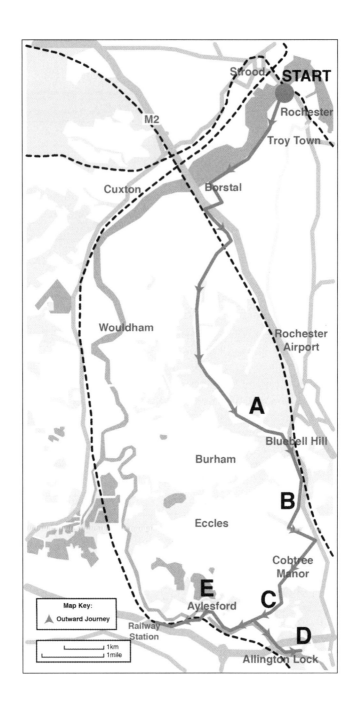

Turn left up the lane immediately after the motorway and follow it for 1km/.6miles.

Turn right, following the North Downs Way sign, up Nashenden Farm Lane.

After 750m/820yds, turn right, following the North Downs Way, via a track and later a lane, for 5.5km/3.4miles to Bluebell Hill (A).

Just before the lane crosses the A229 via a bridge, take the footpath to your right. This is still the North Downs Way, and runs on a mix of hedge-lined tracks and lanes.

After 1.5km/.9miles, Kit's Coty House (B) will be in the field on your right.

500m/550yds after Kit's Coty House, when you meet a road, cross it and then take the footpath, still the North Downs Way, which runs left.

Follow this footpath for 700m/770yds until you reach the A229 again, then turn right.

Follow this path as it first skirts a wood, then runs through it and across fields, reaching a group of houses at Great Crossington after 600m/660yds.

When you reach a T-junction, turn right and pass between the houses at Great Crossington and continue for 400m/440yds.

Look out for a path to the left. There are several options, but take the central one diagonally left and cross the golf course to enter a wood. Pick up the path that runs left, then curves gently right.

After 500m/550yds you are in the grounds of Cobtree Manor. When you reach a tarmacked path, turn right and follow it down through the parkland and out into Forstall Road.

Turn right onto Forstall Road, and continue for 200m/220yds, until you reach a footpath on your left.

Take the footpath down to the River Medway and turn left along the riverbank.

After 1km/.6miles you will arrive at Allington Lock (D).

Retrace your steps along the riverbank, and continue for a total of 2.5km/1.25miles to Aylesford.

Cross the river by the old bridge at Aylesford (E) which is closed to motor traffic.

Turn right after the river and follow the riverside path for 1km/.6miles until a sign points left to Aylesford railway station, which you reach after 50m/55yds.

Walk 9: The home of Pickwickian, and Kent, cricket
West Malling town trail

West Malling is Muggleton in *The Pickwick Papers*. Well, it's half the inspiration for the fictional town where the Pickwickians watch a thrilling game of cricket. Dickens also had Maidstone in mind. Given that he chose to create a fictional name for the place, we can assume Muggleton is a blend of real places, but it is at West Malling (then called Town Malling) that the model for the cricket ground – and for the cricketers' inn, the Blue Lion – are to be found.

As William Hughes points out in his 1891 guide, *A Week's Tramp in Dickens-Land,* his son Charley attested to West Malling's role. Hughes wrote: 'Great weight must be attached to the fact that the present Mr Charles Dickens, in his annotated Jubilee Edition of [*The Pickwick Papers*], introduces a very pretty woodcut of "High Street, Town Malling," with a note to the effect that "Muggleton, perhaps, is only to be taken as a fancy sketch of a small country town; but it is generally supposed, and probably with sufficient accuracy, that, if it is in any degree a portrait of any Kentish town, Town Malling, a great place for cricket in Mr Pickwick's time, sat for it."'

In Chapter seven of *The Pickwick Papers* we learn 'How the Dingley Dell Cricket Club played All-Muggleton, and how All-Muggleton dined at the Dingley Dell expense.'

This is a gentle town stroll, in contrast to our vigorous country walks, and the Swan, inspiration for The Blue Lion – plus numerous other pubs and restaurants – offer great opportunities for lunch. Perhaps come when a cricket match is being played.

In Dickens' time, the pitch at Town Malling was the Kent county cricket ground, and is reputed to be the site of the first recorded match in Kent. In the novel, the Pickwickians travel over from Dingley Dell (Cobtree Hall at Sandling) with their host, Mr Wardle, and meet up again with Alfred Jingle, the actor who speaks in Morse code, who they encountered in Rochester.

As we walk up from the railway station on Swan Street we pass the **home of Silas Norton (A)**, co-founder of Town Malling Cricket club. Just after it is **The Cascade (B),** a remarkable eighteenth-century waterfall that tumbles from the wall of Malling Abbey. The abbey was built by Gundulf, Bishop of

The Cascade in West Malling's Swan Street

Rochester from 1075 to 1108, who also built the cathedral. Malling Abbey is now home to an Anglican order of Benedictine nuns.

The Swan (C) was where the defeated Dingley Dell team stood dinner and drinks for the victorious All Muggleton eleven after the game:

'Within a quarter of an hour all were seated in the great room of the Blue Lion Inn, Muggleton ... There was a vast deal of talking and rattling of knives and forks, and

The Swan, model for The Blue Lion in *Pickwick Papers*

plates; a great running about of three ponderous-headed waiters, and a rapid disappearance of the substantial viands on the table... When everybody had eaten as much as possible, the cloth was removed, bottles, glasses, and dessert were placed on the table; and the waiters withdrew to 'clear away,' or in other words, to appropriate to their own private use and emolument whatever remnants of the eatables and drinkables they could contrive to lay their hands on.'

A riotous night ensured until, a few minutes before midnight, 'the convocation of worthies of Dingley Dell and Muggleton were heard to sing, with great feeling and emphasis, the beautiful and pathetic national air of:

'We won't go home till morning,
We won't go home till morning,
We won't go home till morning,
Till daylight doth appear.'

William Hughes found The Swan to still be a cricketers' inn when he visited in 1898. He wrote: 'the parlour of The Swan... has in it many very fine lithographic portraits of all the great cricketers of the middle of the nineteenth century, including Pilch, Lillywhite, Box, Cobbett, Hillyer (a native of Town Malling)'.

Fuller Pilch, the greatest batsman in the country at the time, and William Hillyer, the principal bowler for Kent, were both star performers at the ground when Dickens was writing *Pickwick*.

When the Pickwickians encounter Alfred Jingle, and they ask him how he came to be in Muggleton, he replies, in his characteristic shorthand: 'Stopping at Crown - Crown at Muggleton – met a party – flannel jackets – white trousers – anchovy sandwiches – devilled kidney – splendid fellows – glorious.'

The Crown may have been The Rose and Crown, which stood at **40 High Street (D)** diagonally right across its junction with Swan Street.

To continue our town stroll, we pass through the 52-acre lake-side **Manor Park (E)**, once part of the eighteenth-century estate created by Thomas Douce, and then past **St Leonard's Tower (F)**, a Norman keep believed to be another of Bishop Gundulf's creations. The cascade we

St Leonard's Tower, where the spring that feeds the Cascade rises

85

West Malling cricket ground, scene of the great game in *Pickwick Papers* and once the Kent country ground

passed earlier is fed from a spring at the foot of the tower.

Dickens described the **Old County Cricket Ground (G)** where, before the game, 'Two or three Dingley Dellers, and All-Muggletonians, were amusing themselves with a majestic air by throwing the ball carelessly from hand to hand; and several other gentlemen dressed like them, in straw hats, flannel jackets, and white trousers – a costume in which they looked very much like amateur stone masons were sprinkled about '

This ground hosted 14 first-class cricket matches between 1836, when Dickens was writing *Pickwick*, and 1890. However, from 1842 Town Malling became too small to hold the large crowds attracted to games, and the Kent County Cricket Club was formed in Canterbury, and that ground took precedence.

THE WALK

What you need to know	
Distance	3.3km/2miles
Time	1 hour (not including stops)
Terrain	Mainly pavements
Map	OS Explorer 148 Maidstone & The Medway Towns
Starting point	West Malling railway station
How to get there	Train to West Malling, or car, parking at the station
Key points along the way	The fixture list for the Town Malling Cricket Club can be found here: http://townmallingcc.play-cricket.com
Refreshments and accommodation	The Swan, Swan Street (drink, food) www.theswanwestmalling.co.uk 01732 521910 Numerous other cafes, pubs and restaurants

Step by step directions

Turn right out of West Malling railway station and walk along Station Approach to Swan Street.

Turn left on Swan Street and walk 300m/330yds, passing Silas Norton's house (A), the Cascade (B) and the Swan Inn, the Blue Lion in Pickwick Papers (C) up to High Street.

Diagonally right across the High Street is The Crown (D) where Alfred Jingle may have lodged.

Turn left on High Street and walk for 500m/550yds, the road becoming St Leonard's Street along the way, and follow the route as it bends left, then right.

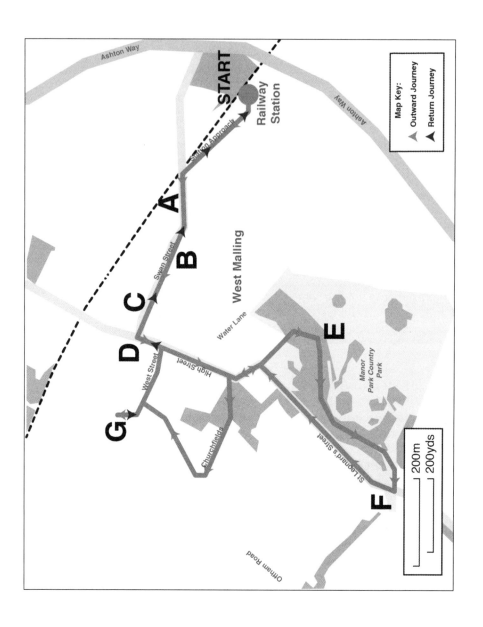

As St Leonard's Street bends right, take the footpath on your left into Manor Park (E).

Follow the path as it runs down to the lake and then bears right along the far side of it for 500m/550yds.

At the end of the lake follow the footpath as it returns to St Leonard's Street. Opposite you is St Leonard's Tower (F).

Turn right on St Leonard's Street and walk for 1.1km/.9miles until you reach St Mary's church.

Take the footpath through the churchyard, emerging in Churchfields.

At the end of Churchfields, in 130m/142yds, turn left into Offham Road.

Follow Offham Road for 300m/330yds, until you reach Norman Road.

Turn left on Norman Road and cross over. The Old County Cricket Ground (G) is on your right after a few metres/yards.

Leaving the cricket ground, turn left into Norman Road, keeping straight on when it becomes West Street, until after 250m/273yds you reach High Street. Turn left into High Street, cross over and in 50m/55yds turn right into Swan Street.

Walk for 250m/273yds down Swan Street to return to the railway station, which will be on your right.

WALK 10: THE CITY OF DAVID COPPERFIELD
CANTERBURY CITY TRAIL

Dickens never lived in Canterbury, but visited the city regularly and knew it intimately. In *David Copperfield*, his favourite and most autobiographical novel, he used many Canterbury locations and buildings, blending and fictionalising them to suit his purpose.

David Copperfield is, in substantial part, a Canterbury novel. The city first appears when David is on his weary trek, escaping London and the misery of working in the bottling factory. He passes through on his way to Dover, and the sanctuary he hopes his aunt Betsy Trotwood will provide.

From this first visit David remembers 'the sunny streets of Canterbury, dozing as it were in the hot light; and with the sight of its old houses and gateways, and the stately, grey Cathedral.'

Later, Canterbury is where Betsy sends David to school, where he encounters the ostensibly 'umble but actually ruthlessly scheming and ambitious Uriah Heep, and where he is reacquainted with the penniless Micawbers.

Dickens' knowledge of Canterbury was noted by Annie Fields, wife of the author's American agent, in her diary. With his characteristic energy and enthusiasm, Dickens took the Fields to many locations that had inspired him – to the extent, Annie confides, that they 'explored the city under Dickens' direction till it was nearly dark'.

Among the places that may have been in Dickens' mind when he wrote David Copperfield is the **House of Agnes (A),** now a B&B, in Dunstan Street. This is one of several buildings that lay claim to be the home of the Wickfield family, where David lodges during his Canterbury schooldays.

Perhaps to bolster its case, it takes its name from Mr Wickfield's

The House of Agnes in Dunstan Street, among the possible models for Mr Wickfield's house in *David Copperfield*

daughter, the dutiful and loyal Agnes, who has been her father's 'little housekeeper' since her mother died. Here, David first encounters Uriah Heep, Wickfield's damp-palmed, reptilian young clerk. Wickfield, a solicitor blighted by alcoholism, almost loses everything to Uriah.

Certainly, there is a local tradition that this is the place Dickens was thinking of, but in terms of physical description, there are stronger candidates, as we shall see a little later on our walk. Even putting Dickens connections aside, the House of Agnes is of interest. There has been an inn here since the thirteenth century. The current building dates from the sixteenth century, and was one of several inns built just outside the West Gate into the city to accommodate travellers who arrived after the nightly curfew, when the gate was locked.

When David O. Selsnick and George Cukor were filming perhaps the best of the many adaptations of the novel, in 1934, they visited the House of Agnes to ensure they captured it in the film, and were photographed at the door.

However, when Dickens was guiding Mr and Mrs Fields around Canterbury, and they tried to guess which of the many crooked houses was the Wickfields', he laughed and told them that several would do. The truth, probably, is that he took elements from several and merged them in his imagination.

Close by, at 35 and 65 North Lane, are two possible locations for **Uriah Heep's ''umble dwelling' (B)**. Both were demolished in 1905. Robert Allbut, in his 1899 guide *Rambles In Dickens Land*, favoured No 65, which he described as 'a small two-storeyed house with a plaster front, on the right side, near the entrance of the lane' which would place it where a car park is now.

There is this description of the interior of the Heeps' house in David Copperfield:

'We entered a low, old-fashioned room, walked straight into from the street, and found there Mrs Heep, who was the dead image of Uriah, only short... It was a perfectly decent room, half parlour and half kitchen, but not at all a snug room. The tea things were set upon the table, and the kettle was boiling on the hob. There was a chest of drawers with an escritoire top, for Uriah to read or write at of an evening; there was Uriah's blue bag lying down and vomiting papers... I don't remember that any individual object had a bare, pinched, spare look, but I do remember that the whole place had.'

Perhaps the strongest candidate for Wickfield's house, in terms of the look of the building, is **The Crooked house (C)** at 27 Palace Street, now a bookshop, and the next point on our walk.

It fits Dickens' description: 'At length we stopped before a very old house bulging out over the road; a house with long low lattice-windows bulging out still farther, and beams with carved heads on the ends bulging out too, so that I fancied the whole house was leaning forward, trying to see who was passing on the narrow pavement below.'

This seventeenth century building's alarming lean was brought about by a chimney shifting, causing the building to tilt perilously. Over the decades the lean got more pronounced until, in 1988, the chimney collapsed. A steel frame was inserted, saving the building and preventing it shifting any further.

A little way along Palace Street is the church of **St Alphege (D)**, where David's headmaster, Dr Strong, marries the much younger Annie Markleham, about whom Uriah Heep spreads vicious and unfounded rumours of unfaithfulness. The church is now de-consecrated, and houses an outfitters' for pupils at the King's School.

In Guildhall Street are two locations of interest. **The Guildhall (E)** now a Costa coffee shop, is where David Copperfield is asked to 'go round to the Guildhall and bring a couple of officers' after it is proved Uriah Heep has been systematically swindling Mr Wickfield.

Fictional Canterbury met the real thing when, a few doors away at the **former Theatre Royal (F)**, now absorbed into Debenhams, Dickens gave a reading of David Copperfield in 1861.

Two inns lay claim to being the place Dickens was thinking of when he had David reunited with the Micawbers, who he had lodged with in London

The Crooked house in Princes Street, another possible model for Mr Wickfield's house in *David Copperfield*

The Sun Hotel lays claim to The Little Inn where Mr Micawber stays in *David Copperfield*

while working at the bottling factory. They are the **Sun Hotel and Little Inn (G)** in Sun Street, and the **Cathedral Gate Hotel (H),** just around the corner in Burgate.

Dickens writes: 'It was a little inn where Mr Micawber put up, and he occupied a little room in it, partitioned off from the commercial room, and strongly flavoured with tobacco-smoke. I think it was over the kitchen, because a warm greasy smell appeared to come up through the chinks in the floor, and there was a flabby perspiration on the walls. I know it was near the bar, on account of the smell of spirits and jingling of glasses.'

Despite the Sun Hotel adding Little Inn to its name, it has no stronger claim to a place in Dickens' imagination than the Cathedral Gate Hotel, which stands beside Christ Church Gate, the main entrance to Canterbury Cathedral.

The cobbled square on which the Cathedral Gate Hotel stands was the **Old Buttermarket (I)**. It may well be here that David and his aunt come on market day, Aunt Betsy 'insinuating the grey pony among carts, baskets, vegetables, and huckster's goods. The hair-breadth turns and twists we made, drew down upon us a variety of speeches from the people standing about, which were not always complimentary; but my aunt drove on with perfect indifference, and I dare say would have taken her own way with as much coolness through an enemy's country.'

It may also have been here that David encountered the fearsomely aggressive butcher's boy 'the terror of the youth of Canterbury'. In Dickens' time there was a famous butcher's shop just off the Buttermarket, at 14 Mercery Lane.

Dickens has David say of him: 'He is a broad-faced, bull-necked young butcher, with rough red cheeks, an ill-conditioned mind, and an injurious tongue. His main use of this tongue is to disparage Dr Strong's young gentlemen... He waylays the smaller boys to punch their unprotected heads, and calls challenges after me in the open streets. For these sufficient reasons I resolve to fight the butcher.'

This does not go well: 'In a moment the butcher lights ten thousand candles out of my left eyebrow. In another moment I don't know... where I am, or where anybody is... At last I awake, very queer about the head, as from a giddy sleep, and see the butcher walking off putting on his coat as he goes, from which I augur justly that the victory is his.'

Dickens knew **Canterbury Cathedral (J)** well. Annie Fields attended Evensong with him during her visit. David Copperfield attended services there regularly; and Mr Micawber had unrealistic aspirations for his son to become a chorister.

The cathedral, its precincts and **The King's School (K)** are well worth visiting. King's lays claim to being the oldest continuously operating school in the world. It was founded in 597 by St Augustine, the first Archbishop of Canterbury, and became The King's School under Henry VIII.

Despite Dickens having indicated that he did not model Dr Strong's Academy on King's, there are clear similarities between the two, in terms of appearance

The King's School bears close similarities to Dr Strong's Academy in *David Copperfield*

and location. Canterbury Historical Society also argue that 'similarities between Dr Strong and the then headmaster, Dr John Birt are striking – they shared an equable temperament, both married late in life to women who were much younger, both loved music'.

Dickens describes the school as 'a grave building in a courtyard, with a learned air about it that seemed very well suited to the stray rooks and jackdaws who came down from the Cathedral towers to walk with a clerkly bearing on the grass-plot.'

At **40 Burgate (L)** is a third house that may have been in Dickens' mind when he described Mr Wickfield's residence. Currently a branch of Fired Earth Interiors, it once housed a firm of solicitors whose names – Plummer and Fielding – appear in Dickens' story *Cricket in the Hearth.*

A fourth claimed Wickfield abode is **Queen Elizabeth Guest Chamber (M)**, a remarkable building at 43-45 High Street, which dates from at least 1200 and which sports a flamboyant painted plasterwork facade. It gets its name from the fact that Elizabeth I stayed here when visiting Canterbury in 1573 and entertained a potential suitor, the Duke of Alençon, in what was then the state room of the Crown Inn. They didn't click, but the encounter is the subject of the satirical song turned nursery rhyme *Froggy Went A Courting.*

THE WALK

What you need to know	
Distance	3 km/1.9miles
Time	45 minutes (not including stops)
Terrain	Pavements and pedestrianised city centre
Map	OS Explorer 150 Canterbury & the Isle of Thanet
Starting point	Canterbury West railway station
How to get there	Train to Canterbury West, or car. Canterbury is notoriously bad for parking. If you want to drive, I suggest you head for a village on the railway line just outside the city, such as Chartham, where you can park in the village hall car park for four hours, and come in one stop (5 minutes) by train
Key points along the way	Canterbury Cathedral www.canterbury-cathedral.org
Refreshments and accommodation	The following have Dickens connections: The House of Agnes, (B&B accommodation) St Dunstan's Street www.houseofagnes.co.uk/ 01227 472185 Sun Hotel and Little Inn, Sun Street (drink, food, accommodation) www.sunhotel-canterbury.co.uk 07527964261 Cathedral Gate Hotel Burgate www.cathgate.co.uk/ 01227 464381

Step-by-step directions

From Canterbury West railway station turn right into Station Road West and walk 200m/220yds up to St Dunstan's Street. Diagonally across to your right at 71 St Dunstan's Street is the House of Agnes B&B (A).

Now turn left on St Dunstan Street and walk 100m/110yds to North Lane. The car park on your right down North Lane is the site of what may have been Uriah Heep's house (B).

Retrace your steps down North Lane, turn left and walk 200m/220yds to The Friars.

Turn left into The Friars and walk 150m/165yds to King Street.

Turn left into King Street and walk 250m/275yds to Palace Street.

At the junction of these two roads, at 27 Palace Street, is The Crooked House (C), among the buildings laying claim to be Mr Wickfield's house.

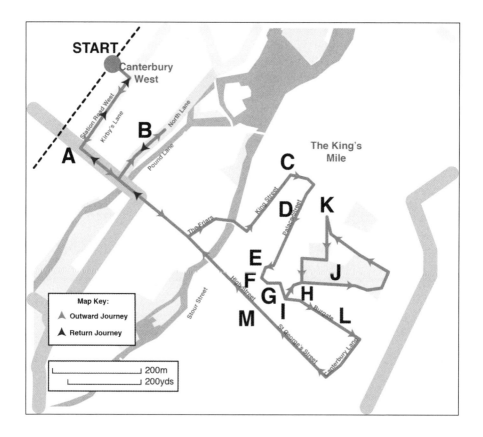

Walk down Palace Street for 100m/110yds and St Alphage (D), now an outfitters to the King's School, is on your right. David Copperfield's headmaster was married here.

Continue for a further 100m/110yds to the junction with Guildhall St.

Turn right into Guildhall Street. Where The Guildhall (E) once stood is now a Costa coffee shop, and the former Theatre Royal (F) is now part of Debenhams.

Turn right just after Debenhams and, after a few metres, you reach Sun Street. The Sun Hotel (G) and the Cathedral Gate Hotel (H) both claim to be the Little Inn from Great Expectations.

This area, in front of the Christ Church Gate entrance to Canterbury Cathedral precincts, is where the Old Buttermarket (I) was once held.

Enter Canterbury Cathedral (J) precincts through Christ Church Gate.

King's School (K) is within the precincts to the north of the cathedral.

Enter the cathedral via the cloister and once you have explored it, leave the precincts via the exit just to the left of Christ Church Gate, and turn left into Burgate.

In 50m/55yds, at 40 Burgate (L), on your left, Fired Earth Interiors is another of the buildings laying claim to be Mr Wickfield's House.

Turn right into Canterbury Lane and walk 100m/110yds to St George's Street.

Turn right into St George's Street and walk 200m/220yds, as it becomes Parade and then High Street, to reach 44 High Street, the Queen Elizabeth Guest Chamber (M).

To return to Canterbury West station, continue for 450m/490yds up High Street, which becomes St Peter's Street, and turn right into Station Road West.

The station is 200m/220yds on your left.

Walk 11: Dickens' Favourite Seaside Resort
Broadstairs Town Trail

Of all the Kent seaside resorts in which Dickens spent his summers, Broadstairs was by far his favourite. From 1837 to 1851 he came almost every year, usually staying from June to October.

He wrote from here to a friend: 'A good sea – fresh breezes – fine sands – and pleasant walks – with all manner of fishing-boats, lighthouses, piers, bathing-machines, are its only attractions, but it's one of the freshest little places in the world.'

Dickens wrote parts of *The Pickwick Papers, Nicholas Nickleby, The Old Curiosity Shop, Dombey and Son, David Copperfield*, and *Bleak House* here. He liked Broadstairs because this 'little fishing-place; intensely quiet; built on a cliff' was old-fashioned and overlooked, and he could work uninterrupted.

He was great friends with James Ballard, the proprietor of the **Royal Albion Hotel (A)** who he described as 'one of the best and most respectable tradesmen in England.' He sold 'good Hollands' gin and, Dickens adds immodestly, 'he has a kind of reverence for me.'

Dickens stayed at the Royal Albion in 1839, and returned three times during the 1840s. At the time, No 40 Albion Street, where he had his rooms, was a house separated from the hotel. It was here that Dickens finished writing *Nicholas Nickelby,*

Royal Albion Hotel, a favourite of Dickens

and he said of No 40 'We enjoy this place amazingly.' By the time he returned for a final visit in 1859, No. 40 had been absorbed into the hotel, and Dickens wrote to his daughters Mamie and Katey, telling them 'I am now (Ballard having added to the hotel a house we lived in three years) in our old dining-room and sitting-room, and [have] our old drawing-room as a bedroom.' If you fancy sleeping in Dickens' bedroom, it is now the hotel's Room 35.

Dickens' first two visits to Broadstairs were in 1837 and 1838, when he was less famous, and too poor to afford the Royal Albion. **Dickens' first lodgings (B)** with his wife Catherine and baby son Charley were in a very modest cottage at 12 High Street, on the site of the shop one door down from Belvedere Road.

William Hughes, in his 1891 guide *A Week's Tramp In Dickens-Land* described it as 'a plain little dwelling of single front, with a small parlour looking into the street, and has one storey over – just the place that seems suited to the financial position of the novelist when he was commencing life. The house is now occupied by Mr Bean, plumber and glazier, whose wife courteously shows us over it... We ask the good lady if she is aware that Charles Dickens had formerly stayed in her house, and she replies in the negative, so we recommend her to get her husband to put up a tablet outside to the effect "Charles Dickens lived here, 1837".'

There is such a plaque today, and another on the greengrocer's next door, beside a broken first-floor window, which reads: 'Charles Dickens lived here. The same time this window was broken.'

Walking through the town along Albion Street we turn into Church Road and pass **Holy Trinity (C)** which Dickens described as 'a hideous temple of flint, like a great petrified haystack'.

On the cliff-top is Dickens' favourite holiday home, **Bleak House (D),** then called Fort House and since greatly extended, and crenelated. John Forster, friend and biographer, wrote of it: 'The residence he most desired stood prominently at the top of a breezy hill... with a cornfield between it and the sea.'

Dickens described his day here in a letter to a friend: 'In a bay window sits from nine o'clock to one, a gentleman with rather long hair and no neckcloth who writes and grins as if he thought he were very funny indeed... At one he disappears, and presently emerges from a bathing machine, and may be seen – a kind of salmon-coloured porpoise – splashing about in the ocean. After that he may be seen in another bay window on the ground floor eating a strong lunch, after that walking a dozen miles or so, or lying on his back in the sand reading a book. Nobody bothers him unless they know he is disposed to be talked to; and I am told he is very comfortable indeed. He's as brown as a berry, and they *do* say is [worth] a small fortune to an innkeeper who sells beer and old punch. But that is mere rumour.'

That innkeeper ran **The Tartar Frigate (E)** which we reach down the steps from Bleak House, on the harbour-side. Dickens wrote that the Tartar Frigate was 'the cosiest little sailor's inn that is to be met around the coast... the very walls have long ago learned *Tom Bowling* and *The Bay of Biscay* by heart and would be thankful for a fresh song'.

Dickens loved to relax at the harbour. In *Our English Watering Place*, a eulogy to Broadstairs, he wrote: 'We have a pier – a queer old wooden pier, fortunately without the slightest pretensions to architecture, and very picturesque in consequence... For ever hovering about this pier, with their hands in their pockets, or leaning over the rough bulwark it opposes to the sea, gazing through telescopes which they carry about in the same profound receptacles, are the boatmen of our watering-place.'

William Hughes met Harry Ford, one of the sailors Dickens befriended. Harry told him: 'I can see old Charley, as we used to call him among ourselves, here a-coming flying down the cliff with a hop, step and jump, with his hair all flying about. He used to sit sometimes on that rail' (pointing to the one surrounding the harbour), 'with his legs lolling about and sometimes on the seat that you're a sitting on now (adjoining the old Look-out House), and he was very fond of talking to us fellows and hearing our tales... He was very good-natured and nobody was liked better.' That seat is still there.

Walking on, up Harbour Street and turning into Fort Road, we pass another of Dickens' holiday homes.

The Tartar Frigate and, on the clifftop behind it, Bleak House

The harbourside bench, to the right of the picture, where Dickens loved to sit

Archway House (F) was called Lawn House when Dickens stayed here in 1841, while writing *Barnaby Rudge*. He described it as 'a small villa between the hill and the cornfield'.

Backtracking a little, we turn into Victoria Parade, where what is now **Chiappini's (G)** cafe was, in Dickens time, Crampton's bath-house. On his final visit, Dickens wrote to daughters Katey and Mamie to say that, because he had a bad cold affecting his throat and chest he couldn't bathe in the sea, and so: 'I get a heavy shower-bath at Mrs Crampton's every morning.'

Tucked behind a little park called Nuckell's Garden is the **Dickens House Museum (H)**. This was the model for Betsy Trotwood's house in *David Copperfield*. It was the home of a formidable lady: Dickens' good friend Mary Pearson Strong, who was the model for David's Aunt Betsy. Betsy takes David in when, his parents dead, he flees London and the bottling factory where he has been put to work.

Miss Strong (and Betsy) waged a constant battle against the boys who allowed donkeys to eat the grass outside her house. In the novel we read:

'To this hour I don't know whether my aunt had any lawful right of way over that patch of green; but she had settled it in her own mind that she had, and it was all the same to her. The one great outrage of her life, demanding to be constantly avenged, was the passage of a donkey over that immaculate spot... Jugs of water, and watering-pots, were kept in secret places ready to

The Dickens House Museum, in what was the model for Betsy Trotwood's house in *David Copperfield*

be discharged on the offending boys; sticks were laid in ambush behind the door; sallies were made at all hours; and incessant war prevailed. Perhaps this was an agreeable excitement to the donkey-boys; or perhaps the more sagacious of the donkeys, understanding how the case stood, delighted with constitutional obstinacy in coming that way.'

Dickens, who loved a practical joke, would sometimes give the donkey man a shilling to provoke a confrontation. He moved Aunt Betsy's cottage to Dover in the novel, but the parlour described in David Copperfield is easily recognisable when you visit today.

Dickens' son Charley, who visited the house with his father, and remembered: 'Miss Strong – a charming old lady who was always most kind to me as a small boy, and to whose cakes and tea I still look back with fond and unsatisfied regret'.

Just beyond the Dickens house is the **Charles Dickens Inn (I)**, which was Nuckell's Library and Assembly Rooms in Dickens' day, and had once been the social centre of Broadstairs.

In *Our English Watering Place*, Dickens pokes gentle fun at this rather dusty institution: 'There is still an Assembly Rooms, a bleak chamber rumoured once to have held concerts and balls, but that is in the dim and distant past. It has a discoloured old billiard table.

'Sometimes, a misguided wanderer of a ventriloquist, or an infant phenomenon, or a juggler, or somebody with an Orrery [a clockwork model of the solar system] that is several stars behind the time, takes the place for a night, and issues bills with the name of his last town lined out, and the name of ours ignominiously written in, but you may be sure this never happens twice to the same unfortunate person...'

But Broadstairs was changing. The old, genteel summer residents had forsaken it, and the railway allowed day-trippers to flood in, altering its character. Dickens complained to John Forster: 'Vagrant music is getting to that height here, and is so impossible to be escaped from, that I fear Broadstairs and I must part company in time to come. Unless it pours of rain, I cannot write half an hour without the most excruciating organs, fiddles, bells, or glee singers. There is a violin of the most torturing kind under the window now (time, ten in the morning), and an Italian box of music on the steps – both in full blast.'

In future, summers would be spent in Folkestone and Dover, which we explore in Walks 14 and 16.

THE WALK

What you need to know	
Distance	2.5km/1.55miles
Time	40 minutes (not including stops)
Terrain	Pavements
Map	OS Explorer 150 Canterbury & the Isle of Thanet
Starting point	Royal Albion Hotel, Albion Street
How to get there	Car, or train
Key points along the way	Dickens House Museum www.thanet.gov.uk/info-pages/dickens-house-museum/ (Closed December to Good Friday)
Refreshments and accommodation	Royal Albion Hotel, Albion Street (drink, food, accommodation) www.albionbroadstairs.co.uk 01843 868071 Tartar Frigate (drink, food) www.tartarfrigate.co.uk 01843 862013 Chiappini's, Victoria Parade (drink, food) 01843 865051 The Charles Dickens pub and restaurant, Victoria parade (drink, food) www.charlesdickensbroadstairs.co.uk pub 01843 600160, restaurant 01843 603040

Step by step directions

From the Royal Albion Hotel (A) go up the High Street for 200m/220yds.

The shop on the left, one door down from Belvedere Road, is where Dickens first stayed in the town (B).

Retrace your steps and turn left in front of the Royal Albion Hotel into Albion Street.

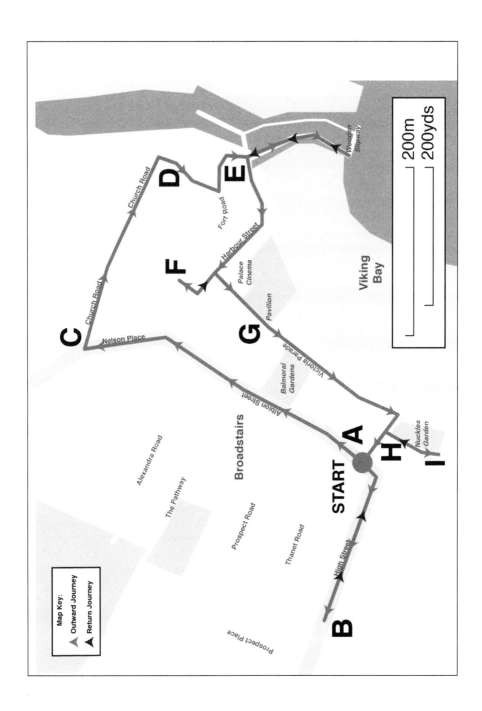

Map Key:
Outward Journey
Return Journey

200m
200yds

Viking
Bay

Church Road

Church Road

Nelson Place

Alexandra Road

The Pathway

Prospect Road

Thanet Road

Prospect Place

High Street

Broadstairs

Albion Street

Balmoral
Gardens

Victoria Parade

Pavilion

Palace
Cinema

Harbour Street

Fort Road

Wooden
Slipway

Nuckles
Garden

START

A
B
C
D
E
F
G
H
I

After 400m/440yds turn right into Church Road. The 'Flint Church' Dickens hated is on the corner (C).

Walk 250m/155yds to the end of Church Road, where Bleak House (D) is on the right.

Turn right past the house and, after 100m/110yds, go left down the steps to the harbour, emerging alongside the Tartar Frigate (E) in Harbour Street.

Explore the pier and then return to Harbour Street.

After 150m/165yds turn right into Fort Road, in front of the Old Curiosity Shop, to see Archway House (F). It was called Lawn House when Dickens stayed here.

Retrace your steps to Harbour Street, turn left then almost immediately right onto the path that leads to Eldon Place. Chiapinnis (G) was once the bath house, frequented by Dickens.

Continue straight for a further 200m/220yds as Eldon Place becomes The Parade. The Dickens House museum (H) is on your right just after the Royal Albion Hotel, and the Charles Dickens pub is just beyond it (I).

After visiting one or both of these, turn left to return to your starting point at the Royal Albion Hotel.

Walk 12: Dickens' daily clifftop walk
Broadstairs to Ramsgate and back

The bracing stride out along the cliffs or sands from Broadstairs to Ramsgate was a favourite with Charles Dickens. While he valued the peace and quiet he found at Broadstairs, his love of crowds, fun and spectacle meant the more boisterous resort of Ramsgate held a strong attraction for him.

This was one of his regular daily walks, once the morning's writing was accomplished, offering the option of taking the cliff top or, for most of the way and at low tide, walking along the beach or promenade.

In 1837 he wrote to a friend: 'I have walked upon the sands at low-water from this place to Ramsgate, and sat upon the same at high-ditto till I have been flayed with the cold. I have seen ladies and gentlemen walking upon the

Viking Bay, Broadstairs, from the promenade where our walk begins

earth in slippers of buff, and pickling themselves in the sea in complete suits of the same, I have seen stout gentlemen looking at nothing through powerful telescopes for hours, and, when at last they saw a cloud of smoke, fancying a steamer behind it, and going home comfortable and happy.'

In an early short story, *The Tuggses at Ramsgate*, Dickens vividly captured the scene in 1836 – before the railway came to the town – as a steam packet from London delivered its cargo at Ramsgate's **East Pier (A)**:

Ramsgate's Royal Harbour

'The sun was shining brightly; the sea, dancing to its own music, rolled merrily in; crowds of people promenaded to and fro; young ladies tittered, old ladies talked; nursemaids displayed their charms to the greatest possible advantages; and their little charges ran up and down and to and fro under the feet and between the legs of the assembled concourse... There were old gentlemen trying to make out objects through long telescopes, and young ones making objects of themselves in open shirt collars; ladies carrying about portable chairs, and portable chairs carrying about invalids; parties waiting on the pier for parties who had come by the steam boat and nothing was to be heard but talking, laughing, welcoming, and merriment.'

Dickens himself would often be among such a crowd as he lined up to take the boat to the city, or when meeting friends arriving for a stay with him at Broadstairs.

The Tuggses are a family of Cockney greengrocers who have suddenly come into a fortune, and decide it is time to go up in the world. So they do what the middle-classes do, and head to the seaside for the summer months, rejecting Gravesend: 'low'; and Margate: 'nobody here but tradespeople' for slightly superior Ramsgate. Where they get swindled out of a chunk of their newly acquired riches by a posh conman.

Dickens packs everything he had observed of holidaymaking in Ramsgate into the story. There is the scene on the sands where the ladies 'were employed in needlework, or watch-guard making, or knitting, or reading novels; the gentlemen were reading newspapers and magazines; the children were digging holes in the sand with wooden spades, and collecting water therein; the nursemaids, with their youngest charges in their arms, were running in after the waves, and then running back with the waves after them;

and, now and then, a little sailing-boat either departed with a gay and talkative cargo of passengers, or returned with a very silent and particularly uncomfortable-looking one.'

There was the novel sport of sea bathing, Mr Tuggs watching as 'four young ladies, each furnished with a towel, tripped up the steps of a horse-drawn bathing-machine. In went the horse, floundering about in the water; round turned the machine; down sat the driver; and presently out burst the young ladies aforesaid, with four distinct splashes.'

The view of Harbour Parade from Ramsgate's harbour

And in the evenings, there were the libraries – actually all-purpose places of entertainment offering food and drink, music, modest gambling, and people-watching: 'There were marriageable daughters, and marriage-making mammas, gaming and promenading, and turning over music, and flirting. There were some male beaux doing the sentimental in whispers, and others doing the ferocious in moustache.'

Dickens also enjoyed the vibrant popular culture he found in Ramsgate. He attended George Sanger's Amphitheatre, where circus and music hall acts played. Paul Schlicke, in *Dickens and Popular Entertainment,* writes that, in 1846, Dickens 'was caught in a "whirl of dissipation" upon discovering a female lion tamer,' Ellen Chapman, soon to become Sanger's wife. 'He wrote to [a friend] "That you should have been and gone and missed last Saturday! Wild beasts, too, in Ramsgate, and a young lady in armour, as goes into dens, while a rustic keeper who speaks through his nose exclaims, 'Behold the abazid power of woobbud!'"

'Seriously,' Dickens went on, 'she beats van Amburgh [an American animal trainer who had developed the first trained wild animal act]. And I think the Duke of Wellington must have her painted by Landseer.'

The Amphitheatre was replaced by a supermarket in 1960, but if you fancy a diversion into Ramsgate town centre, you'll find directions below.

THE WALK

What you need to know	
Distance	9.5km/6miles
Time	2 hours 30 minutes (not including stops)
Terrain	A mix of grass, and tarmacked paths. Short, steep descent into Broadstairs, stairs up the cliff on your return
Map	OS Explorer 150 Canterbury & the Isle of Thanet
Starting point	Broadstairs seafront
How to get there	Car, or train to Broadstairs. Station is 600m/660yds from the seafront
Refreshments and accommodation	Albion Hotel, Albion Street (drink, food, accommodation) www.albionbroadstairs.co.uk 01843 868071 Morelli's ice cream and coffee bar, Victoria Parade Broadstairs http://www.morellisgelato.com/ 01843 862500 Beach kiosk (drink, food) on the route at Dumpton Gap Italianate Glasshouse Tea Garden (drink, food) open Monday to Friday, April to September plus weekends during fine weather. On the route in King George IV Park www. italianateglasshouse.co.uk 07868 722060 Royal Harbour Brasserie (drink, food) at the far end of East Pier, Ramsgate www.royalharbourbrasserie.co.uk 01843 599059

Step-by-step directions

Walk west out of Broadstairs for 300m/330yds along Victoria Parade, following the path over Louisa Gap.

Continue for 200m/220yds to Western Esplanade.

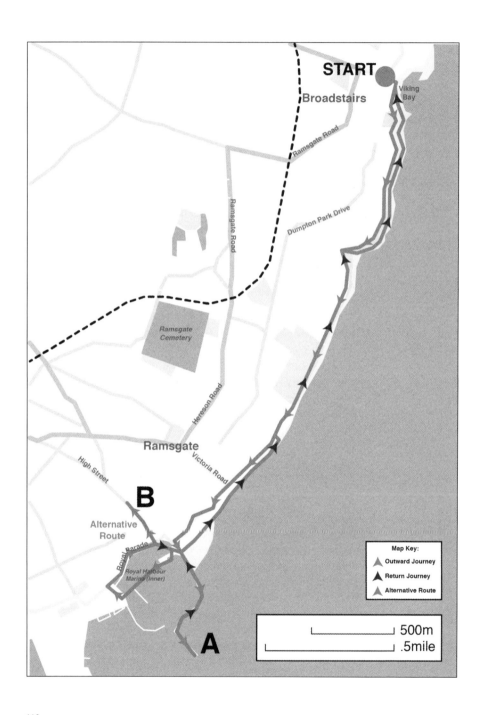

START

Broadstairs

Viking Bay

Ramsgate Road

Ramsgate Road

Dumpton Park Drive

Ramsgate Cemetery

Hereson Road

Ramsgate

Victoria Road

High Street

B

Alternative Route

Royal Parade

Royal Harbour Marina (inner)

A

Map Key:

▲ Outward Journey

▲ Return Journey

▲ Alternative Route

500m

.5mile

After1.5km/.9miles the path rounds Dumpton Gap and continues for a further 1km/.6miles alongside South Cliff Parade.

Carry on, through George VI Park, to emerge after 350m/380yds on the edge of Ramsgate at Victoria Parade.

Continue along the clifftop for 1.1km/.7miles past Wellington Crescent and descend on Madeira Walk until, after 1.1km/.7miles, you reach a passageway on the left leading between buildings down to the harbour.

Turn left and walk along Harbour Parade for 100m/110yds.

Turn right for East Pier.

Retrace your steps, turning left just before Harbour Parade and walking for 600m/660yds on East Crosswall, then continuing on to West Crosswall, the piers between the inner and outer marinas, to cross to the western side of the harbour.

[Note, at high tide, the bridge allowing you to walk right across the harbour may be raised, in which case, if you want to explore the harbour, you will have to keep straight on at the bottom of Madeira Drive on to Royal Parade, taking the left fork onto Military Road.]

Turn right, and right again into Military Road.

Note: to see the spot where Sangar's Amphitheatre stood (B) see 'Alternative route' below.

Follow Military Road for 400m/440yds to return to Harbour Parade. Turn right into Harbour Parade.

Take the seafront path at the end of Harbour Parade and follow it for 1.4km/.9miles until you see a path on your left sloping up the cliff to Winterstoke Gardens.

Leave the seafront promenade at this point.

Turn right at the clifftop and retrace your steps for 1km/.6miles until you reach Dumpton Gap.

Turn right, following the green footpath sign down to the beach at Dumpton Gap.

Follow the lower promenade for 1km/.6miles back into Folkestone.

Alternative route

To see the site of Sangar's Ampitheatre (B), turn left (instead of right for Harbour Parade), into Harbour Street, which becomes High Street, and walk for 400m/440yds to the junction with George Street. The venue was on the corner of these two roads. To return to the main route, retrace your steps to Harbour Parade.

Walk 13: Where Dickens' Mistress Made a New Life
Broadstairs to Margate
and Margate Town Trail

This splendid walk, spanning a string of sandy bays and airy clifftops, is a perfect summer hike. What's more, our destination, Margate, is one of the least expected treasure houses of Dickens' personal story. It was here that his mistress Ellen Ternan created a new life for herself after his death.

Dickens had met Ellen Lawless Ternan, known as Nelly, in 1857, when she was 18 and he was 45. Ellen's father was dead, and her mother and sisters were struggling to make a living in the theatre. Dickens took them under his wing, seeking to further their careers, especially Nelly's.

In a coincidence that will have seemed highly significant to Dickens, Nelly was born in Rochester, a city that had played a crucial part in his childhood, and where he returned to live in middle age. (See Walk 4: Rochester city trail.)

Kingsgate Bay, one of a string of bays we pass on our walk to Margate

He and Nelly embarked on a 13-year affair, during which Dickens abandoned his wife, and which only ended on his death. Although their relationship was never publicly acknowledged – Dickens' reputation would never have survived the revelation that such a pillar of the community was unfaithful – the author's family and friends were well aware of it.

When her lover died, Nelly was in a terrible position. Quite apart from overwhelming grief at her loss, Dickens had housed her, in Peckham, and funded her completely. The prospects for a bereaved mistress in Victorian England were dire. Yet Nelly was able to achieve a remarkable reinvention of herself, in which her past was erased. She dropped her age, incredibly, by 14 years – from 37 to 23 – and in 1876, six years after Dickens' death, she married George Robinson, a clergyman and Oxford graduate 12 years her junior who knew nothing of her relationship with Dickens.

With George, Nelly came to Margate, where they ran a school, a private boarding establishment they named **Margate High School (A)**, off Hawley Street, where there is now a Morrison's supermarket. The couple became pillars of Margate society, and had a son, Geoffrey, and a daughter, Gladys. Claire Tomalin, in her biography *The Invisible Woman*, commented: 'By her boldness – the boldness she had observed in Dickens and learnt from him – she had achieved the ambition of the right-minded Victorian girl.'

Nelly always acknowledged Dickens as a friend of the family, but as she had dropped her age so drastically, she would appear to have been little more than a child at the time of his death.

In a sign of how closely Nelly was still connected with Dickens' family, his sister-in-law Georgina Hogarth – for many years the author's besotted housekeeper – stayed with Nelly for a week's summer holiday in Margate in 1877.

George became a magistrate, and Nelly returned to the stage, in *An Evening with Dickens*, featuring readings and recitations from *A Christmas Carol, Nicholas Nickleby, David Copperfield* and *Bleak House.* She appeared at the **Theatre Royal (B)** in Hawley Square before Christmas 1885 in an adaptation of *The Old Curiosity Shop.*'

Perhaps unknown to her, Dickens had visited this theatre regularly in the years he summered in Broadstairs,

The Theatre Royal Margate, which Dickens attended and where Ellen Ternan performed

which had no theatre of its own. Her own father trod these boards, and her own children would attend theatre school here. Yet Nelly kept secret the fact that, from childhood until she became Dickens' lover, she had been a professional actress.

There was, however, one person Nelly confided in in Margate: her priest, the Revd William Benham of **St Johns Church (C)**. We know that because, years later, he broke the seal of the confessional and passed her confidences on to a Dickens biographer.

Claire Tomalin writes: 'She told him, it seems, that she had been Dickens' mistress; that he had set her up [in a house]; that he had visited her two or three times a week; that she had come to feel remorse about her relations with

St John's, Margate. Nelly confided in its vicar that she had been Dickens' mistress

him during her lifetime, and that her remorse had made them both miserable; and that she now "loathed the very thought of this intimacy". It may be that Nelly had become pregnant by him in April 1867, when the words 'arrival' and 'loss' appear in Dickens' diary. There may have been other pregnancies.

In another coincidence, this area of Margate has a connection with Dickens before he met Nelly. The area off the High Street, in front of St John's, was called Six Bells after a notorious pub of that name. This was a slum area, and the primitive cesspool drainage contaminated the wells, causing outbreaks of cholera. It was also a place of prostitution.

Dickens was a passionate social reformer, and in London was involved with a charity to assist what were then known as fallen women. In Margate, his interest appeared to be not solely in such women's welfare. In 1841 he wrote to his friend Daniel Maclise describing the joys of Margate, and commented 'there are conveniences of all kinds at Margate (do you take me?) And I know where they live'.

Sadly, Ellen Ternan's new life in Margate was not to last. Seven or eight years after her arrival, the school failed, her husband George suffered a breakdown, and the couple moved to a succession of addresses in suburban London. Nelly died in 1914.

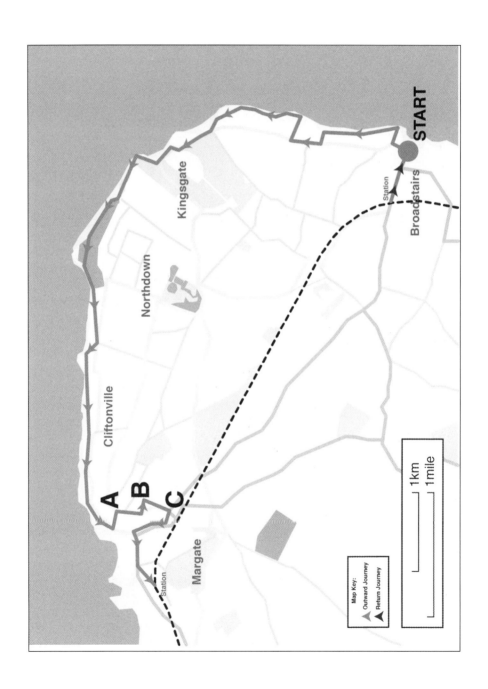

START

Broadstairs

Station

Kingsgate

Northdown

Cliftonville

A
B
C

Margate

Station

Map Key:
Outward Journey
Return Journey

1km
1mile

THE WALK

What you need to know	
Distance	10.4km/6.5miles
Time	2 hours 30 minutes (not including stops)
Terrain	Mainly grass and gravel paths, and pavements in town
Map	OS Explorer 150 Canterbury & the Isle of Thanet
Starting point	Royal Albion Hotel, Albion St, Broadstairs
How to get there	Car, or train to Broadstairs. Note: Return by train from Margate to Broadstairs
Refreshments and accommodation	Broadstairs: Albion Hotel, Albion Street (drink, food, accommodation) ww.albionbroadstairs.co.uk 01843 868071 Morelli's, Victoria Parade Broadstairs (drink, food) www.morellisgelato.com 01843 862500 The Captain Digby, Kingsgate Bay (drink, food) www.captaindigby.co.uk 01843 867764 Margate: Walpole Bay Hotel, Fifth Avenue (drink, food, accommodation) www.walpolebayhotel.co.uk 01843 221703 Turner Contemporary Cafe, The Rendezvous 01843 233000 Cupcake Cafe, Market Place (drink, food) 01843 231598

Step-by-step directions

From the Royal Albion Hotel, walk east along Albion Street for 400m/440yds. Turn right into Church Road. Turn left when you reach the cliffs.

Follow the cliff-top path and then Eastern Parade for 800m/880yds.

Turn left when Eastern Parade meets Park Road.

At the end of Park Road, in 100m/110yds, turn right into Stone Road.

Follow Stone Road, which becomes North Foreland Road, for 300m/330yds.

Turn right into North Foreland Avenue and almost immediately bear right into Cliff Road, following it for 200m/220yds until you reach the cliff top.

Turn left into Cliff Promenade, continue for 900m/990yds to the end of the road, then go on through the car park until you meet Joss Gap Road.

Cross Joss Gap Road and turn right into the footpath on the opposite side.

When this path ends in 300m/330yds there is a 100m/110yds stretch where you must cross over and walk in the road. Take care!

Follow the road through Kingsgate Bay for 300m/330yds.

Turn right into the footpath just beyond the Captain Digby pub.

Follow the coastal footpath for 3.8k/2.4miles into Margate.

Pass the Turner Contemporary gallery on your right then, 200m/220yds later, turn right into High Street.

Almost immediately, bear left into Market Street.

Follow Market Street for 160m/175yds to Hawley Street.

Turn right into Hawley Street and cross over.

Morrison's supermarket is on the site of Margate High School (A).

Continue along Hawley Street for 250m/275yds to Hawley Square.

Turn left into Hawley Square. The Theatre Royal (B) is on your left at the far end, after 100m/110yds.

Turn right into Addington Street and follow it for 150m/165yds until it meets St John's Street.

Continue straight on along St John's Street for 50m/55yds until it joins Churchfields.

St Johns Church (C) is on your left after 80m/88yds.

Cross Churchfields opposite the church and go along High Street for 400m/440yds until you reach Marine Gardens.

Turn left into Marine Gardens and follow it for 450m/490yds to reach Margate railway station.

Return to Broadstairs by train.

At Broadstairs station turn left into High Street and follow it for 500m/550yds back to the Royal Albion Hotel.

WALK 14: THE PORT DICKENS CAME TO LOVE
DOVER TOWN TRAIL

Dover is a place where most people have been, but only to get on or off a cross-channel ferry, and have rarely stopped to look around. At first sight the town is unprepossessing, but it really is worth a closer look. The Dickens connections are strong, and bring to life an older, affluent, and imposing Dover.

Dickens first came here as part of a theatrical troupe in the 1830s. From 1844, when the railway arrived, he used it frequently when crossing to Boulogne where his sons were at boarding school, and in the 1850s and 60s

The view from Western Heights, Dover, where Dickens lay down to write, and admire the view

spent long periods here. In 1852 he wrote of it, 'the sea is very fine, and the walks are quite remarkable'.

We cover two of those remarkable walks: one going east to Deal, the other west to Folkestone, in Walks 15 and 16.

Dover features in *A Tale of Two Cities* and *David Copperfield*, and Dickens also wrote a good deal of *Bleak House, Little Dorrit* and *The Uncommercial Traveller* here. *A Tale of Two Cities* contains an atmospheric description of Dover:

'The little narrow, crooked town of Dover hid itself away from the beach, and ran its head into the chalk cliffs, like a marine ostrich. The beach was a desert of heaps of sea and stones tumbling wildly about, and the sea did what it liked, and what it liked was destruction. It thundered at the town and thundered at the cliffs, and brought the coast down madly.'

It is to Dover, and his Aunt Betsey Trotwood, that David Copperfield flees after his mother dies and his stepfather puts him to work in a London bottling factory.

Although the model for Betsy Trotwood – and her home – were actually in Broadstairs, and covered in Walk 11, the house's actual location is in Dover. By the time he wrote *David Copperfield*, in 1848-9, Dickens was falling out of love with Broadstairs, his holiday home from 1837-51, and chose to set significant segments of the novel in his new favourite place.

It took David Copperfield six days to walk to Dover from London. The anticipation had been enormous, but 'when I stood with my ragged shoes, and my dusty, sunburnt, half-clothed figure, in the place so long desired, it seemed to vanish like a dream, and to leave me helpless and dispirited.' He asks first the boatmen, then the fly (horse-drawn cab) drivers and shopkeepers, for directions to his aunt's house, but none will help him.

Finally, 'I was sitting on the step of an empty shop at a street corner, near the market-place... when a fly-driver, coming by with his carriage, dropped a horsecloth. Something good-natured in the man's face, as I handed it up, encouraged me to ask him if he could tell me where Miss Trotwood lived.'

That shop, until recently the Dickens' Corner Restaurant, is at **7 Market Square (A)**.

The fly driver does help, saying: '"If you go up there," pointing with his whip towards the Heights, "and keep right on till you come to some houses facing the sea, I think you'll hear of her. My opinion is she won't stand anything, so here's a penny for you."'

Thanks to Lorraine Sencicle (doverhistorian.com), who has researched the route David must have taken, we can follow in his footsteps. David walks along Queen Street to Cowgate Hill.

To David's left, actually set sideways-on to the sea, is a row of **pilots' cottages (B)** lived in by the seamen who guided ships in and out of Dover

Harbour. One cottage in the centre of the row, occupied by the senior pilot, is larger. This was the location, but not the model, for Aunt Betsey's house, and the row of cottages are now sheltered housing. We visit the actual house described in *David Copperfield* (as opposed to its location) in Walk 11.

Just beyond the cottages, a flight of 80 steps leads up Western Heights, a vast hilltop fortification and garrison dating from the 1800s, from which, on a clear day, there are wonderful views of France. At the foot of the steps was **Pilots' Field (C)**, then a meadow let out for grazing, now allotments. In the last decade of his life, Dickens would often come here during fine weather and write, lying on the grass.

There are also panoramic views of Dover's various harbours. The

The shop at 7 Market Square, where David Copperfield rested after his six-day trek from London

modern ferry harbour is to the east, but right below Western Heights are the nineteenth century piers and docks that Dickens would have known. Our walk takes us through the fort and down South Military Road to Lord Warden Square, and **Lord Warden House (D)** which, as the Lord Warden Hotel, became Dickens' favourite place to stay in the town.

The brief given in 1853 to architect Samuel Beazley, a leading designer of theatres, was to create a hotel that looked 'magnificent from the sea, the barracks [on Western Heights] and for passengers coming by rail. It was named after the Duke of Wellington, in his role of Lord Warden of the Cinque Ports, who had died the previous year.

This then-grand hotel, now offices, was alongside **Admiralty Pier (E)** and the former harbour railway station. Admiralty Pier now houses Cruise Terminal Two, but you can walk through the long, covered walkway that led passengers from train to ship, and out onto the pier, from the end of which you get a wonderful view of the busy port. In Dickens' time, the Lord Warden had a private corridor leading directly to the walkway from the hotel's first floor.

Before switching to the Lord Warden, Dickens stayed at the Ship Inn, on the harbourside overlooking **Custom House Quay (F)**. Long demolished, we pass the spot where the Ship stood as we approach Dover Marina.

Dickens escaped to the Ship Inn in 1856, when things were dire at his London home, Tavistock House, where his infuriating in-laws the Hogarths had temporarily moved in with him, and his marriage was in trouble. He stayed at the Ship Inn from 15 March to 23 May, while trying to write the sombre novel *Little Dorrit*.

The former Lord Warden Hotel, now offices, became Dickens' favourite on his many trips through Dover

However, agitation over his private life and the distractions from his window made it impossible to concentrate. In an essay, *Out Of The Season*, published in the magazine *Household Words* in June 1856, he telescoped his two-month stay into three days, writing: 'It fell to my lot, this last bleak Spring, to find myself in a watering-place out of the Season. A vicious north-east squall blew me into it from foreign parts, and I tarried in it alone for three days, resolved to be exceedingly busy. On the first day, I began business by looking for two hours at the sea and staring the Foreign Militia out of countenance. Having disposed of these important engagements, I sat down at one of the two windows of my room, intent on doing something desperate in the way of literary composition, and writing a chapter of unheard-of excellence – with which the present essay has no connexion...

'I had scarcely fallen into my most promising attitude, and dipped my pen in the ink, when I found the clock upon the pier – a red-faced clock with a white rim – importuning me in a highly vexatious manner to consult my watch, and see how I was off for Greenwich time.'

We pass that **clock tower (G)** next.

His watch put right, Dickens finds another distraction: 'It was impossible, under the circumstances, for any mental resolution, merely human, to dismiss the Custom-house cutter, because the shadow of her topmast fell upon my paper, and the vane played on the masterly blank chapter. I was therefore under the necessity of going to the other window; sitting astride of the chair there, like Napoleon bivouacking in the print; and inspecting the cutter as she lay, all that day, in the way of my chapter.'

Finally, he gives up, and decides to go on a 10-mile hike to Deal, the same route we take in Walk 15.

Dickens also took houses for long summer visits in Dover, staying regularly at **17 Waterloo Crescent (H)** one of two adjoining houses on the harbour front owned by the artist Lambert Weston, who had his studio in No 18. In July 1852, he stayed nearby at **10 Camden Crescent (I)**.

This section of the Crescent was destroyed during the Second World War, but the last surviving house now bears a plaque marking Dickens' stay nearby. His friend and collaborator Wilkie Collins, author of *The Woman In White*, came to stay with him, and wrote an account of the highly regulated way Dickens organised the household. The regime was: Breakfast at 08.10 hours, afterwards writing until 14.00 hours then walking. Dinner was at 17.30 hours and bed between 22.00-23.00 hours.

Camden Crescent, where Dickens stayed with Wilkie Collins

On our way back to the railway station we cross under Snargate Street. Close to here was the **Apollonian Hall (J)**. Dickens was part of an acting troupe that played here in the 1830s. From 1857 he gave regular public readings at the hall from his novels, and it became a favourite venue. He wrote after one performance:

'The audience with the greatest sense of humour is certainly Dover. The people in the stalls see the example of laughing, in the most curiously unreserved way; and they laughed with such cordial enjoyment... that the contagion extended to me. For one couldn't hear them without laughing too.'

In 1861 a Snargate Street draper, John Agate, wrote angrily to Dickens after failing to get seats at the Apollonian for his family. Dickens wrote to apologise, and Agate put the letter up in his shop window. The Apollonian was demolished in 1929 during a dock redevelopment scheme.

THE WALK

What you need to know	
Distance	8.8km/5.5miles
Total ascent	97m/318ft
Time	2 hours (not including stops)
Terrain	Mainly flat, on pavements. One sharp ascent to Western Heights, followed by a gentle descent
Map	OS Explorer 138 Dover, Folkestone & Hythe
Starting point	Dover Priory railway station
How to get there	Train to Dover Priory railway station, or car
Refreshments and accommodation	Dover Marina Hotel, Waterloo Crescent (drink, food, accommodation) www.dovermarinahotel.co.uk 01304 203633

Step-by-step directions

From Dover Priory Station walk out to Folkestone Road, turn left and cross over.

After 200m/220yds, at the roundabout turn right into York Street, then cross over at the lights.

Continue down York Street for 100m/110yds, then turn left into New Street.

At the end of New Street turn right into Cannon Street.

At the end of Cannon Street is Market Square. The empty shop outside which David Copperfield sat (A) is on your left as you enter the square, on the corner of Castle Street.

Leave Market Square via King Street, bearing right into Queen Street after 50m/55yds.

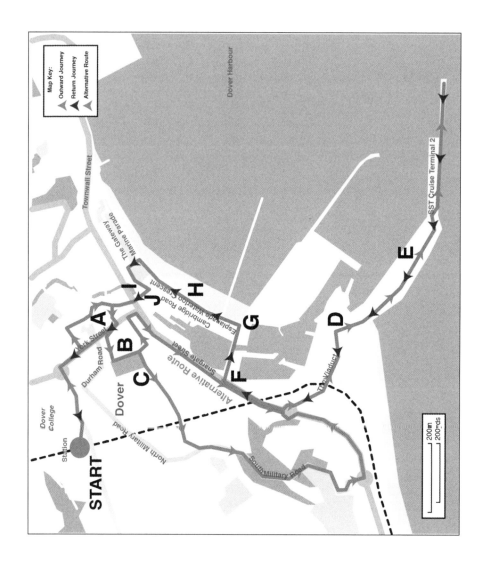

Map Key:
Outward Journey
Return Journey
Alternative Route

Dover Harbour

SST Cruise Terminal 2

Townwall Street

The Gateway
Marine Parade

Cambridge Road
Esplanade Waterloo Crescent

Snargate Street

Viaduct

Alternative Route

Dover

Dover College

York Street

Durham Road

Station

START

North Military Road

South Military Road

A
B
C
D
E
F
G
H
I
J

200m
200yds

Where Queen Street joins York Street, turn right and cross over.

After 30m/33yds turn left up a footpath leading to Cowgate Hill.

The terrace to your left as you approach the graveyard is the location of Betsy Trotwood's house in *David Copperfield* (B).

Where Cowgate Hill turns sharp left, follow it for 100m until you reach a footpath going off to the right.

NOTE: The route from here passes through the fort on Western Heights. The route is open during daylight hours. If you are concerned the route may not be open, an alternative is offered at the end of this section.

Follow this footpath for 170m/185yds up steps to Western Heights (C), where you reach a fort.

Follow the path left and down into the fort.

Turn left, then, after you round a corner, look out for a small doorway on your left, which leads through the outer wall of the fort.

Turn right and join Drop Redoubt Road.

Follow Drop Redoubt Road for 150m/165yds until it joins North Military Road.

Turn left into North Military Road, which becomes Centre Road, then South Military Road, and walk for 350m/380yds to join the A20.

Turn left along the A20 for 600m/660yds.

Cross the A20 at the lights just after a roundabout, from which you will see The Viaduct leading off to your right. Turn back to reach The Viaduct.

Follow The Viaduct for 400m/440yds to reach Lord Warden House, formerly Dickens' favourite Lord Warden Hotel (D).

Turn right behind the former hotel, then right immediately after it to find the entrance to Admiralty Pier (E). Walk through the covered way to the open pier.

Retrace your steps back down The Viaduct to the A20 (here called Snargate Street) and turn right.

After 200m/220yds, at the next roundabout, turn right into Union Street. The site of the Ship Inn (F), is on your right immediately after you turn.

After 100m/110yds the clock tower (G) is in front of you.

Turn left into Esplanade which becomes Waterloo Crescent. After 400m/440yds, Dickens' lodgings at 17 Waterloo Crescent (H) are on your left.

Continue on Waterloo Crescent for a further 200m/220yds to Wellesley Road.

Turn left into Wellesley Road then, after 50m/55yds, turn left into Camden Crescent (I).

Continue along Camden Crescent then almost immediately right on to New Bridge. Close to here was the Apollonian Hall, were Dickens read (J).

Take the underpass beneath the A20 (here called Townwall Street).

In 100m/110yds turn left into Queen Street, which leads to York Street.

Turn right into York Street, cross over and walk 300m/330yds to the roundabout.

At the roundabout, take the left turn up Folkstone Road.

After 200m/220yds, Dover Priory railway station is off to your right.

Alternative route avoiding Western Heights
From Cowgate Hill continue straight on to join Adrian Street.

At the end of Adrian Street, turn right into York Street, then right again onto the A20.

Follow the A20 for 600m/660yds until you reach The Viaduct, then pick up the directions above.

Walk 15: The very edge of England
Dover to Deal

This is a wonderful walk: a scramble uphill behind Dover's poundingly busy port to reach the top of the wonderful White Cliffs, then a great swooping route along the very edge of England.

Up here you quickly put yourself a world away from the endless string of trucks filing into the bellies of the great channel ferries lined up far beneath you.

For close on 17.4km/10.8miles you are on top of the world, with just a refreshing dip down into St Margaret's Bay, before regaining the heights. Then, after another inspiring stretch away from it all, there is the gentle descent to the wide pebble beach on the approach to Deal – the 'town without a cliff' as Dickens referred to it.

The view across the harbour from Dover's East Cliff

He knew Deal well. In his Broadstairs years he paused in Deal on his walks to Dover. Later, when staying at Dover in spring 1856, and struggling to write *Little Dorrit*, he took the walk we follow here to try to clear his head. He wrote about it in an essay, *Out Of The Season*, published in *Household Words* in June that year. And, as he says there, he enjoyed it so much that he retraced his steps the following day.

Dickens walked there and back both days, but I suggest a return to Dover by train from Deal.

He was certainly made of tough stuff. He made his two round trips in pretty grim weather, the wind 'blowing stiffly from the east'. On the cliff tops he 'overtook a flock of sheep with the wool about their necks blown into such great ruffs that they looked like fleecy owls. The wind played upon the lighthouse [by which he means the **South Foreland Lighthouse (A)**, which we pass] as if it were a great whistle, the spray was driven over the sea in a cloud of haze, the ships rolled and pitched heavily, and at intervals long slants and flaws of light made mountain-steeps of communication between the ocean and the sky.'

Once off the cliffs and approaching Deal he observed how: 'On the beach, groups of storm-beaten boatmen, like a sort of marine monsters... stood leaning forward against the wind, looking out through battered spy-glasses.'

Dickens used Deal for one of the settings of his 1852-3 novel *Bleak House*. It is where Esther Summerson comes when visiting Richard Carstone who, like her, is a ward of Mr Tulkinghorn. Tulkinghorn is a lawyer involved in the interminable inheritance case of Jarndyce vs Jarndyce which is the central theme in the novel, and in which the central characters' fates are bound up.

The beach we walk along here is recognisable from Dickens' description of what Esther finds at Deal: 'The long flat beach, with its little irregular houses, wooden and brick, and its litter of capstans, and great boats, and sheds, and bare upright poles with tackle and blocks, and loose gravelly waste places overgrown with grass and weeds, wore as dull an appearance as any place I ever saw. The sea was heaving under a thick white fog; and nothing else was moving but a few early ropemakers, who, with the yarn twisted round their bodies, looked as if, tired of their present state of existence, they were spinning themselves into cordage.

Richard Carstone is stationed at **The Royal Marine Depot (B)**, which we pass on the outskirts of Deal. Carstone is terribly in debt and has decided to give up his commission, putting all his hopes in a pay-out from the Jarndyce vs Jarndyce case. Esther hopes to persuade him not to. She and her maid, Charley, stay at the seafront **Royal Hotel (C)**, which is where Dickens often stopped for refreshment, and where I suggest you take a break today.

In *Bleak House* Dickens wrote: 'when we got into a warm room in an excellent hotel and sat down, comfortably washed and dressed, to an early breakfast (for it was too late to think of going to bed), Deal began to look more cheerful. Our little room was like a ship's cabin, and that delighted Charley very much. Then the fog began to rise like a curtain, and numbers of ships that we had had no idea were near appeared. I don't know how many sail the waiter told us were then lying in the downs [the calm waters on the landward side of the treacherous Goodwin Sands]. Some of these vessels were of grand size – one was a large Indiaman just come home; and when the sun shone through the clouds, making silvery pools in the dark sea, the way in which these ships brightened, and shadowed, and changed, amid a bustle of boats pulling off from the shore to them and from them to the shore, and a general life and motion in themselves and everything around them, was most beautiful.'

Dickens also wrote about the Royal Hotel in *Out Of The Season*, but disguises it as the Admiral Benbow. On the occasion of his blustery spring walk he finds a welcome far colder than the one Esther received: 'The parlour

Fishing boats drawn up on the shingle beach approaching Deal

bell in the Admiral Benbow had grown so flat with being out of the season, that neither could I hear it ring when I pulled the handle for lunch, nor could the young woman in black stockings and strong shoes, who acted as waiter out of the season, until it had been tinkled three times.'

The menu is limited: 'Admiral Benbow's cheese was out of the season, but his home-made bread was good, and his beer was perfect,' and the bar is cold because 'deluded by some earlier spring day which had been warm and sunny, the Admiral had cleared the firing out of his parlour stove, and had put some flower-pots in – which was amiable and hopeful in the Admiral, but not judicious: the room being, at that present visiting, transcendently cold.'

Fed up of shivering in the cold bar, he looked out across the stone passage and saw a kitchen with the fire roaring and a high settle pulled up before it: 'I strolled in, bread and cheese in hand, munching and looking about. One landsman and two boatmen were seated on the settle, smoking pipes and drinking beer out of thick pint crockery mugs – mugs peculiar to such places, with parti-coloured rings round them, and ornaments between the rings like frayed-out roots.'

THE WALK

What you need to know	
Distance	17.4km/10.8miles
Time	5 hours 40 minutes (not including stops)
Terrain	Generally well maintained footpaths, but those on the cliffs can be muddy and slippery in wet weather. Long steady climb out of Dover, steep ascent up steps from St Margaret's Bay
Map	OS Explorer 138 Dover, Folkestone & Hythe for most of route, and OS Explorer 150 Canterbury & the Isle of Thanet for final approach to Deal
Starting point	Dover Priory railway station
How to get there	Train to Dover Priory, or car. Return by train from Deal
Refreshments and accommodation	Dover: Dover Marina Hotel, Waterloo Crescent, Dover (drink, food, accommodation) www.dovermarinahotel.co.uk 01304 203633 Along the route: Cafe (in summer season) at South Foreland lighthouse (drink and food) The Coastguard pub at St Margaret's Bay (drink, food) thecoastguard.co.uk. 01304 853051 Deal: The Royal Hotel, Beach Street, Deal (drink, food, accommodation) www.theroyalhotel.com 01304 375555

Step-by-step directions

From Dover Priory railway station bear left into Folkestone Road. After 200m/220yds turn right into York Street.

After 350m (380yds) turn left onto Townwall Street, the A20.

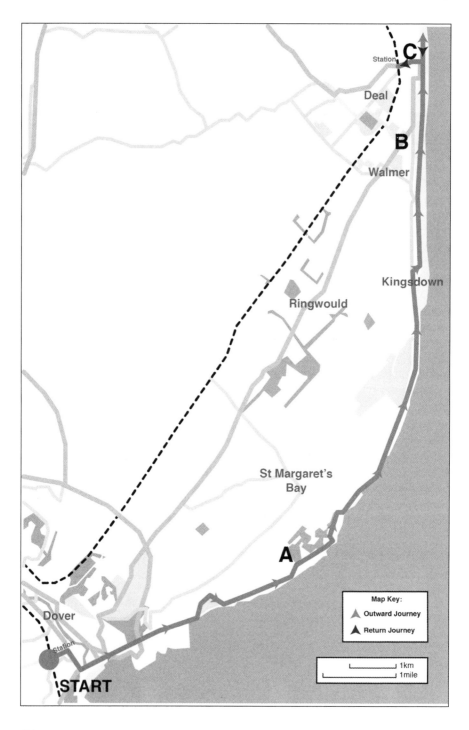

Map Key:
▲ Outward Journey
▲ Return Journey

└──────┘ 1km
└──────┘ 1mile

After 400m (440yds) take a left off the main road, then immediately right into East Cliff.

From here you will pick up signs for the England Coast Path and Saxon Shore Way. These signs alternate, but following them will keep you on the right track.

East Cliff leads to Athol Terrace, which leads to a footpath that ascends the East Cliff and passes the National Trust's White Cliffs visitor centre.

Immediately after the National Trust centre, the path skirts inland, keeping to the high ground above Langdon Bay, then returning to the cliff edge, reaching the South Foreland lighthouse (A) after 1.8km/1.1miles.

Just after the lighthouse the path turns left then, after 200m/220yds, right and picks up a track which, after 1.2km/.75miles, turns sharp left then, after 200m/220yds, sharp right. After 500m/550yds turn right on the road down to St Margaret's Bay.

The path out of St Margaret's Bay is signposted in a patch of trees on your left before the houses at the far end of the beach. Several flights of concrete steps take you back to the cliff top.

After 1.8km/1.1miles of gentle descent, the path reaches a road running parallel with the shingle beach.

Turn right down one of the shingle roads, then left at the path which runs along the beach.

The Royal Marine Depot (B) is on your left after 4km/2.5miles.

The Royal Hotel (C) is a further 1km/.6miles, on your right, on Beach Street.

For the railway station, retrace your steps down Beach Street for 300m/330yds, then turn right into Queen Street.

The station is 400m/440yds down this road.

WALK 16: A CLIFFTOP WALK 'LOVELY AND STRIKING IN THE HIGHEST DEGREE'

FOLKESTONE TO DOVER AND FOLKESTONE TOWN TRAIL

Dickens wrote that the cliff-top walk from Dover to Folkestone was 'lovely and striking in the highest degree', running as it does over 'a chain of grass-covered hills of considerable elevation [which] are enchantingly fresh and free.'

He wrote to friend and collaborator Wilkie Collins of how, jokingly referring to himself in the third person, he 'had taken to expend his superfluous vitality in a swarming up the face of a gigantic and precipitous cliff in a lonely spot overhanging the wild sea-beach. He may generally be seen (in clear weather) from the British Channel, suspended in mid-air with his trousers very much torn, at fifty minutes past 3pm.' Elsewhere Dickens wrote of the great energy such walks gave him: 'daily on the neighbouring downs and grassy hill-sides, I find that I can still in reason walk any distance, jump over anything, and climb up anywhere'.

The view of Dover, from Western Heights

This walk is a stupendous one, climbing hard out of Dover and then following the roller-coaster rise and fall of the downs, and hugging the cliff-top all the way to Folkestone.

Folkestone was one of Dickens' regular holiday resorts after 1851, when the old favourite of Broadstairs became too noisy. In 1853 he stayed at the Pavilion Hotel while writing *A Child's History of England*, and returned in 1855, renting a cliff-top villa. As well as these long stays he made many shorter visits to the town. His sons were at boarding school at Boulogne, and it was easy to visit them from here. They joined him in Folkestone during their summer holidays. From 1862 Dickens used Folkestone as a base to visit his

The approach to Folkestone along the cliffs

mistress Ellen Ternan, who was banished to France at that time so as not to tarnish his reputation. Some accounts suggest she conceived a child, which did not live, while he visited her there.

Dickens wrote about Folkestone in an essay called *Out of Town*, published in *Household Words*, in which he gave it the name Pavilionstone, after the town's Pavilion Hotel. Folkestone had been transformed, in the decade before Dickens started holidaying here, from a little fishing village into a major port. The railway arrived in 1843, and the steamer service to France began a year later.

Out of Town is a persuasive advertisement for the place. Dickens writes: 'our situation is delightful, our air is delicious, and our breezy hills and downs, carpeted with wild thyme, and decorated with millions of wild flowers, are, on the faith of a pedestrian, perfect... And, if you want... to breathe sweet air which will send you to sleep at a moment's notice at any period of the day or night, or to disport yourself upon or in the sea, or to scamper about Kent, or to come out of town for the enjoyment of all or any of these pleasures, come to Pavilionstone.'

The **Pavilion Hotel (A)** played an important part in the transformation of Folkestone. Dickens writes: 'The lion of Pavilionstone is its Great Hotel... you get out of the railway carriage at high-water mark. If you are crossing by the boat at once, you have nothing to do but walk on board and be happy there if you can – I can't. If you are going to our Great Pavilionstone Hotel... you walk into that establishment as if it were your club; and find ready for you your news-room, dining-room, smoking-room, billiard-room, music-room, public breakfast, public dinner twice a day (one plain, one gorgeous), hot baths and cold baths.'

The original hotel stood until 1899, when it underwent a major refurbishment. Today just a small section, attached to the rather less glamourous Grand Burstin Hotel, survives. The rest of the building was demolished in 1981-2.

In 1855, Dickens rented 3 **Albion Villas (B)**, while writing *Little Dorrit*. Uncharacteristically, he was suffering writer's block or, perhaps, finding the wonderful view from his window too much of a distraction. He complained, in a letter, 'I walk downstairs once in every five minutes, look out of the window once in every two, and do nothing else'.

Perhaps it was the view that distracted him. He writes of how: 'on a bright September morning, among my books and papers at my open window on the cliff overhanging the sea-beach, I have the sky and ocean framed before me like a beautiful picture. A beautiful picture, but with such movement in it, such changes of light upon the sails of ships and wake of steamboats, such dazzling gleams of silver far out at sea, such fresh touches on the crisp wave-tops as they break and roll towards me – a picture with such music in the billowy rush upon the shingle, the blowing of the morning wind through the corn-sheaves where the farmers' waggons are busy, the singing of the larks, and the distant voices of children at play – such charms of sight and sound as all the galleries on earth can but poorly suggest.'

Albion Villas, Folkestone, where Dickens stayed

In early October, having just completed the third instalment of *Little Dorrit*, Dickens recited *A Christmas Carol* at Folkestone, in a carpenter's shop on the Dover Road, but not before a stand-off with the townsfolk. Both the high-brow Harveian Literary Institute and the proletarian Working Men's Educational

Dickens' local, the British Lion, in The Bayle, Folkestone

Union had asked for a reading. Dickens said he could only do one, and requested the Harveians, who had asked first, to allow the working men in on affordable terms. They resisted, saying that everyone must pay five shillings. Finally, at Dickens' insistence, the working men were allowed in at threepence.

Just around the corner from Albion Terrace, in The Bayle, is **The British Lion (C)**, Dickens' local during his long visit, and where today they have a Dickens corner dedicated to him.

From 1862, Dickens used Folkestone for his clandestine trips to France – trips he described as 'perpetual' – to visit Ellen Ternan, possibly at Condette, near Boulogne. These trips, lasting days or weeks, have led to a theory that Ternan gave birth to a child by him, a boy who lived only a few months. Claire Tomalin writes, in *The Invisible Woman*: '"there was a boy but it died" – or so said Dickens' son Henry.'

Tomalin adds that, from 1862-65: 'Nelly now disappears from view completely, conjured into thin air. For four years she remains invisible.' She and her mother even miss her sister's wedding in London in 1863. She only reappears in public when she and Dickens are involved in a serious train crash near Staplehurst, in Kent, which we visit in Walk 17.

THE WALK

What you need to know	
Distance	14.8km/miles /9.2miles
Time	5 hours 20 minutes (not including stops)
Terrain	Mainly rough paths over grassland. Steep climb out of Dover
Map	OS Explorer 138 Dover, Folkestone & Hythe
Starting point	Dover Priory railway station
How to get there	Train to Dover Priory, or car, parking at the railway station. Return to Dover by train
Refreshments and accommodation	Dover: Dover Marina Hotel, Waterloo Crescent (drink, food, accommodation) www.dovermarinahotel.co.uk 01304 203633 Folkestone: Ward's Hotel, Earl's Avenue (drink, food, accommodation) 01303 251478 http://www.wardshotel.co.uk/ 01303 245166 The British Lion, 8-10 The Bayle (drink and food) There are also numerous pubs and restaurants alongside Folkestone's harbour

Step-by-step directions

From Dover Priory Station walk out to Folkestone Road, turn left and cross over. After 200m/220yds take the steps on your right leading up to Military Road.

Turn right into Military Road and follow it for 800m/880yds.

Take the path on your right signposted England Coast Path.

These signs plus, at times, signs for Saxon Shore Way and North Downs Way appear on our route. England Coast Path signs are most reliable for keeping to our route.

Follow the path for 700m/770yds as it crosses beneath Western Heights and then descends to run through a small housing development and passes under the A20.

Emerging the other side of the A20, follow the path as it climbs out of Dover, keeping close to the cliff edge.

Follow the path for 5km/3.1miles.

At a sign saying the path ahead goes only to a viewpoint, turn right and, after 50m/55yds, turn left into New Dover Road.

After 200m/220yds take the left fork into Old Dover Road.

After 50m/55yds you will be able to rejoin the England Coast Path, which is just over the grass verge to your left.

After 2.2km/1.4miles take the left-hand path where you see a sign saying you are entering The Warren Country Park.

After 600m/660yds the path joins a lane, and then, after 100m/110yds, leads into Wear Bay Road.

Turn left into Wear Bay Road and follow it for 1km/.6miles.

Where the England Cost Path sign points left, follow it down to the seafront and turn right along the shoreline.

After 800m/880yds the Grand Burstin Hotel, site of Dicken's favourite Pavilion Hotel (A) will be on your left.

Pass to the right of the hotel and walk up Road of Remembrance for 300m/330yds.

At the top, turn right into Albion Villas (B). Dickens' former home, No 3, bears a plaque.

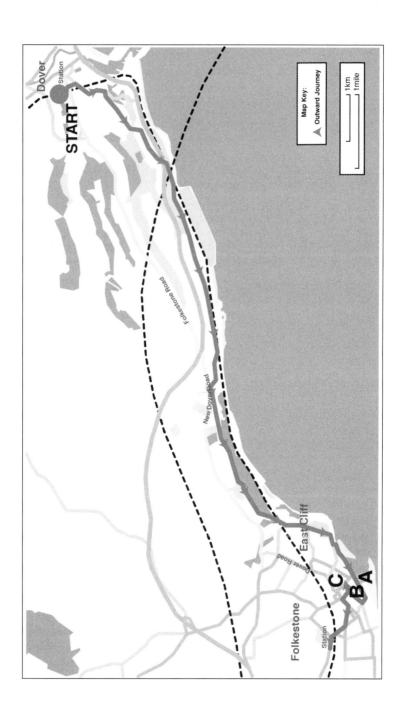

Leaving Albion Villas, turn right into Pound Way then right again, after 100m/110yds, into West Cliff Gardens.

Walk to the end of West Cliff Gardens, then through the churchyard of St Mary and Eanswythe, and continue straight on into The Bayle.

Dickens' local, the British Lion (C) is 50m/55yds down on the right.

Leaving the British Lion, turn left and follow The Bayle to Church Street.

Turn right into Church Street, and keep straight on when, after 200m/220yds, it joins Rendezvous Street.

Keep straight on again when Rendezvous Street joins Guildhall Street.

After 400m/440yds Guildhall Street ends at Shallon Street.

Cross over Shallon Street and turn left.

At the roundabout, bear right into Cheriton Road.

Follow Cheriton Road for 350m/380yds, then bear right at the crossroads to keep on Cheriton Road.

After a further 200m/220yds, pass under the railway bridge and turn left for Folkestone Central station.

Walk 17: The place that changed Dickens' Life
Headcorn and Staplehurst circuit

This walk is different to any of the others in this book: it's one Dickens never took. Its significance is that it passes the scene of the Staplehurst rail crash, an accident in which Dickens could very easily have been killed, and which blighted the last five years of his life.

In 1865 Dickens was returning from Boulogne with his mistress Ellen Ternan and her mother. The Folkestone to London boat train derailed while crossing the Beult viaduct, between Headcorn and Staplehurst, killing 10 and injuring 49. Dickens was terrified of the scandal that would result if he and Ternan were linked at the crash, yet still tended the injured and nursed the dying.

Headcorn village

If that all sounds a bit morbid, please don't be put off. This is a lovely stretch of Kent countryside, and this walk, through farmland and water meadows, is a fine one. It makes a wonderful round trip between Headcorn and Staplehurst. Alternatively, you can walk either half of the overall route, using the train between Headcorn and Staplehurst to return to your starting point.

St Peter and St Paul, Headcorn

It is on our outward route that, close to Boarden Farm, a track leads down to the **crash site (A).** Through fields with crops housed in poly-tunnels we walk to reach a small wood and the viaduct – little more than a bridge over the slow-flowing River Beault.

It was 11 minutes past three in the afternoon of 9 June 1865 that the boat train from Folkestone was approaching the spot, at 50 miles an hour on a downhill gradient. The *Kentish Gazette* reported that a gang of eight platelayers and carpenters, under their foreman Henry Benge, had ripped up a 42-foot length of track and wooden supports that needed replacing. They had been working in the area for 10 weeks, and were well used to working in the gaps between trains, and having the rails back in place in good time. Henry Benge checked the timetable, and thought he saw that he had two hours to get the work completed. Nevertheless, he sent signalman John Wiles along the line with a red warning flag.

Two things were wrong. The first: Benge, barely literate, had misread the timetable and the train was fast approaching. The second, Wiles had not been trained, and didn't know that detonators should be used to alert engine drivers. Also, he had not moved far enough down the track. Which meant that, although the driver of the train saw him waving his warning flag, he did not have time to stop the train, and it was still travelling at between 20 and 30 miles per hour when it hit the gap in the rails.

Eight carriages plunged 15 feet into the muddy river and two more were left hanging from the side of the bridge. *The Gazette* reported: 'The groans of the dying and wounded, the shrieks of frantic ladies and the shrill cries of young children rising from the wreck of the train, and mingling with the hissing of the steam from the engine, were awful in the extreme.'

All but one of the seven first class carriages fell, the exception being the one that Dickens, Ternan and her mother were in. That, still attached by its coupling to the second-class carriage before it, was left hanging over the bridge at a sharp angle, its occupants hurled into a corner.

By Dickens' own account, he went to the door of the carriage and, seeing two of the workmen, told them that if they sent assistance, he would empty his carriage. Using a makeshift arrangement of planks he got Nelly and her mother out, and then saw the other first-class carriages lying in the river bed. He went back into his carriage, took his top hat and a flask of brandy and, filling the hat with water, clambered down the bank to assist the injured.

Seeing one man with his skull cut open, he poured water over his face and gave him a sip of brandy, then laid him on the riverbank. But the man, who was past saving, said 'I am gone,' and died. Next, Dickens saw a woman propped against a tree, her face covered in blood. He gave her brandy and moved on to help others. When he passed her again, she too was dead.

The crash site

A contemporary artists' impression of the crash that Dickens endured

Dickens helped another man, newly married, who was desperately searching for his wife. An eyewitness said 'Dickens led him to another carriage and gradually prepared him for the sight. No sooner did he see her corpse than he rushed round a field at the top of his speed, his hands above his head, and then dropped fainting.'

Dickens continued to help the wounded until an emergency train arrived to take the survivors on to London. Just as he was about to leave, he remembered that the manuscript for the latest instalment of *Our Mutual Friend* was still in the pocket of his overcoat, which he had left in the carriage. He clambered in to retrieve it.

Dickens said that, during his rescue efforts he was 'not in the least flustered' but, once home, he felt 'quite shattered and broken up'. The immediate effect was that he lost his voice for a fortnight, and could not bear to travel at more than walking pace when his son picked him up in a carriage to drive him the mile to his home, Gad's Hill Place, from his local station at Higham. He later told the landlord of his local, the Sir John Falstaff Inn, 'I never thought I should be here again'.

His fear of speed was to persist, and when travelling by train he got the strong sensation that his carriage was dipping down as it had in the accident, leading him to avoid train travel whenever possible. Even three years later he said 'I have sudden vague rushes of terror, even when riding in a hansom cab, which are perfectly unreasonable but quite unsurmountable.'

His daughter Mamie said 'we have often seen him, when travelling home from London, suddenly fall into a paroxysm of fear, tremble all over, clutch the arms of the railway carriage, large beads of perspiration standing on his face, and suffer agonies of terror'.

Another source of terror was that, in the reporting of the crash and the inquest that was to follow, Dickens relationship with Ellen Ternan might be exposed. He wrote to the stationmaster at Charing Cross asking if items including a seal engraved 'Ellen' had been recovered from the crash, and – despite being an important witness – managed to avoid giving evidence at the inquest, after which Henry Benge was sentenced to nine months hard labour.

Even Dickens' heroism was downplayed. *The Kentish Gazette*, in its long report, gave only two sentences to his role. Elsewhere, after initial reports of his helping the wounded, his presence was hushed up.

Peter Ackroyd, in his biography, *Dickens*, suggests that Ellen Ternan may have been 'injured or in some way deeply disturbed by the train crash; from this time forward he tends to call her in his letters "the Patient" and in later life she suffered from intermittent bad health which her friends believed to have been caused in an "accident"; in particular her upper left arm seems to have been a constant source of pain and uneasiness.'

In a postscript to *Our Mutual Friend*, Dickens wrote of how his characters Mr and Mrs Boffin 'were on the South-Eastern Railway with me, in a terribly destructive accident. When I had done what I could to help others, I climbed back into my carriage – nearly turned over a viaduct, and caught aslant upon the turn – to extricate the worthy couple. They were much soiled, but otherwise unhurt... I remember with devout thankfulness that I can never be much nearer parting company with my readers for ever than I was then, until there shall be written against my life, the two words with which I have this day closed this book: – THE END.'

Dickens died five years to the day after the accident.

The experience found its way obliquely into his fiction the following year, in a horror story called *The Signal-Man*. The man, who works in a signal box on a lonely stretch of line, becomes haunted by an apparition. His box is one of a string, along which warnings of any danger on the line are passed via telegraph and alarms. Three times he receives phantom warnings that only he can hear, followed by the appearance of the apparition, and a terrible accident.

THE WALK

What you need to know	
Distances	Headcorn to Staplehurst: 6.9km/4.3miles Staplehurst to Headcorn: 7.5km/4.7miles
Time (not including stops)	Headcorn to Staplehurst: 1 hour 25 minutes Staplehurst to Headcorn: 1 hour 35 minutes
Terrain	Mainly narrow paths over grassland and through woods, which can be muddy in wet weather, plus a number of stretches on generally quiet country lanes
Map	Unfortunately this route spans two maps: OS Explorer 137 Ashford (for Headcorn) OS Explorer 136 High Weald (for Staplehurst)
Starting point	Headcorn railway station. Return possible by train from Staplehurst
How to get there	Train to Headcorn, or car, parking at the railway station
Refreshments and accommodation	Headcorn: George and Dragon, High Street (drink, food) 01622 890 239 Near Staplehust: The Hawkenbury, Hawkenbury Road, just off our route (drink, food, accommodation) www.thehawkenbury.com 01580 890567 Staplehurst: King's Head, High Street (drink, food) www.kingsheadstaplehurst.co.uk 01580 891231

Step-by-step directions

Headcorn to Stapehurst

Turn right out of Headcorn railway station into Station Road and walk 400m/440yds through the village to St Peter and St Paul's church.

Take the path through the churchyard, bearing right after the church and past houses up to Moat Road.

Turn left into Moat Road and walk for 900m/990yds to the point where the road takes a right-angle turn right.

Take the footpath through woods that leaves the road on the outside of that bend.

With the river Beault on your left, walk for 1km/.6miles to reach Kelsham Farm.

Turn right past the farm buildings then take the footpath that goes off to your left just after it, skirting a pond, then turning left, then right, before running on a farm track at the edge of a field.

Follow the track for 600m/660yds to Boarden Farm.

Bear slightly left past the farm buildings.

Just past the buildings a track turns left and runs for 700m/770yds along a field margin, with a hedge to your left, then bears right, reaching the point at which the railway crosses the river Beault, where the accident happened (A).

Retrace your steps back up this track, then turn left and continue for 700m/770yds to come out into Hawkenbury Rd.

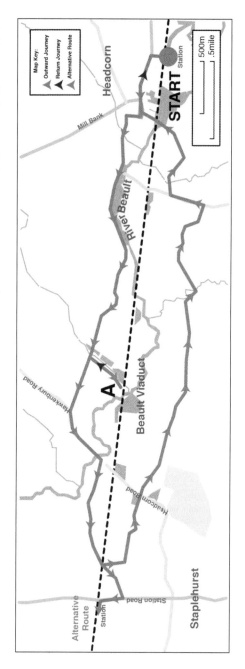

Turn left on Hawkenbury Road and walk for 600m/660yds. A few metres after crossing a river via Hawkenbury Bridge, take the footpath on the right.

Follow the footpath for 250m/275yds across a field, then cross a stile into a wide grassy area and bear left, then right, and cross a field.

In the next field, walk diagonally left to pass, after 200m/220yds, just to the right of Turley Farm buildings.

Follow the farm's drive to come out into Couchman Green Lane.

Turn right into Couchman Green Lane then, after 20m/22yds, take the footpath on the left, which skirts a sewage works then turns left to cross the railway lines.

Caution: Take great care as you cross the tracks: Stop, look, listen for trains coming in either direction.

If you are going to Staplehurst station
Follow the path as it meets Fishers Road.

After 300m/330yds, when Fishers Road meets Station Road, turn right, cross over and turn left to reach Staplehurst railway station.

To continue the circular walk and return to Headcorn.

Take the footpath signposted to the left just after you pass over the railway tracks.

Follow this path through a new housing estate, turning right after 100m/110yds, then left after 300m/330yds to reach a Y junction. With Couchman Green Lane to your left, and Pile Lane to your right, go straight ahead along Sweetlands Lane.

Follow Sweetlands Lane for 400m/440yds until it reaches Headcorn Road.

Cross Headcorn Road and follow the footpath straight ahead for 350m/380yds.

When a lane (Chickenden Lane) is visible through a gap in the hedge to your right, switch over to follow it.

Follow Chickenden Lane for 1.6km/1mile until you reach Chickenden Farm.

Here the lane ends and a wide grassy bridleway continues straight ahead, to the right of the farm buildings.

Caution: Take care on the next short section of the walk between Chickenden Farm and Place Farm. The bridleway is reduced to a footpath, with the way poorly marked, before joining another bridleway after Place Farm.

Here's what you do:
50m/55yds after passing Chickenden Farm, where the main path goes left at a right angle, cross right into the next field and follow the field margin to your left. This section can be badly overgrown and you may have to step over the low, poorly maintained fence and continue just inside the field.

After 200m/220yds, when you reach the next corner of the field, go straight on, passing through the hedgerow to emerge in another field.

Here again, take care not to go wrong.

Diagonally to your right you will see a metal barred gate in a hedgerow. Tack right until you are lined up with that gate, then walk straight towards it.

That way, you will find a bridge over the stream that meanders through this field.

After the gate, a track takes you right through Place Farm and on past Headcorn Place to emerge, after 800m/880yds, in Water Lane.

Turn left into Water Lane. After 250m/270yds, take the footpath to your right which leads, after 300m/330yds, to New House Lane.

Turn right into New House Lane and walk for 200m/220yds until you see a footpath sign pointing to your left.

This path leads, after 700m/770yds, to St Peter and St Paul church.

Enter the churchyard and turn right, emerging in Headcorn's main street.

Walk back through the village for 400m/440yds to Headcorn railway station.

A CHARLES DICKENS BIOGRAPHY
AND SUMMARIES OF THE BOOKS FEATURED
IN THE WALKS IN THIS GUIDE

Charles John Huffam Dickens, to give him his full name, was born in Portsmouth in 1812, to Elizabeth, wife of John, a pay clerk in the Navy. He was the second of eight children.

The family moved to London when Charles was three, then on, briefly, to Sheerness before settling in Chatham, where Charles lived from the ages of four to 11. When the family moved back to London in 1822, Charles stayed for some months to finish his schooling.

John Dickens was a spendthrift, and the family had left mounting debts in Kent. In London, in 1824, creditors caught up with him, and he was sent to the Marshalsea Prison for debtors, where he was joined by his wife and their youngest children, but not Charles.

Charles was set to work in a blacking factory, where shoe and stove polish were manufactured. Even after a windfall meant his father was released from prison, his mother advocated that Charles remain at the factory, a cause of great bitterness for him. He was finally able to return to school for two years after which, aged 16, he became a junior clerk in a law office. Dickens taught himself shorthand in the evenings, and through a relative got a job as a court reporter. He loved theatre, went to performances almost every night, and almost became an actor, but missed the audition because of a cold.

Instead, his journalistic career thrived. In 1835 the *Morning Chronicle* launched an evening edition, edited by George Hogarth, who invited Dickens to write sketches – colourful pieces about people and places – under the pen-name Boz. Charles became a regular visitor to Hogarth's house, where he met his daughter, Catherine. They married in 1836, which was a very big year for Dickens. The success of a collection of his journalism, *Sketches by Boz*, led to an offer to write the text for illustrations which became *The Pickwick Papers*, both of which were published in 1836. The first of the couple's 10 children, Charley, was born in 1937.

Despite having lived in London for 15 years, Dickens' love of Kent remained strong. From 1937 the family spent several months each summer at one of the county's seaside resort: for many years Broadstairs, followed by Dover and Folkestone. In 1857 he bought a house, Gad's Hill Place at Higham, a few miles from his childhood haunts of Rochester and Chatham.

The move coincided with the decision to abandon his wife, which he did with great cruelty, effectively banishing her from their house and demanding that the children take his side or hers. At around the same time he began an affair with a young actress called Ellen Ternan, known as Nelly, which continued until the end of his life. He died, aged 58, on 9 June 1870.

Summaries of the books featured in the walks

Sketches by Boz, 1836

These sketches, described by the publisher as 'Illustrative of Every-day Life and Every-day People' gave Dickens his first success as a writer. They were published in a number of newspapers and journals from 1833 to 1836. They came out in book form in 1836, the same year his first serialised novel, *The Pickwick Papers*, appeared in hard cover. One of the best sketches is *The Tuggses In Ramsgate*, a cautionary tale of a newly-rich Cockney family who get ripped off by a posh conman and woman in the resort.

Sketches by Boz features in Walk 12.

The Pickwick Papers, 1836

Samuel Pickwick and his friends, the amorously susceptible Tracy Tupman, sentimentally poetical Augustus Snodgrass, and would-be sportsman Nathaniel Winkle ramble around the country, with many of their comic adventures taking place in Rochester, Chatham, Cobham and in lightly-fictionalised versions of Maidstone, Sandling and West Malling. The novel opens in Rochester, with adventures including Mr Winkle being challenged to a duel by Dr Slammer, and the Pickwickians getting caught between two advancing armies during a military display on the Great Lines at Chatham. There they meet Mr Wardle, who invites them to his house at Dingley Dell (Cobtree Hall near Sandling) and with whom they go to watch a cricket match between Dingley Dell and All-Muggleton at Muggleton (West Malling). When Tracy Tupman is thrown into depression after the maiden aunt who he has proposed to spurns him to elope with the itinerant actor and charlatan Alfred Jingle, he finds solace in The Leather Bottle, Cobham.

Pickwick locations feature in Walks 1, 2, 3, 4, 5, 8 and 9.

David Copperfield, 1850

David Copperfield's happy childhood is rocked by the death of his father, and destroyed when his easily manipulated mother marries the harsh Mr

Murdstone. The only light in his life, once his mother's affection is cut off from him, is provided by their servant, Peggotty. When his mother dies, David is set to work in a bottling factory, but flees to his aunt Betsy Trotwood in Dover. She organises his education in Canterbury, where he meets the permanently indebted Wilkins Micawber. David then trains in the law in London, where he meets his old schoolfriend Steerforth, who he takes to visit the Peggottys in their house in an upturned boat at Great Yarmouth. Steerforth shocks David by eloping with Little Emily, David's childhood playmate at the Peggotys'. David marries the child-like Dora Spenlow but, while finding success and then fame as a writer, Dora's health – and his love for her – is failing.

Meanwhile, Uriah Heep has managed to supplant his boss, the alcoholic Wickfield, and is plotting to persuade his daughter, Agnes, to marry him. Agnes, however, is concealing her love for David Copperfield, and resists Heep. Mr Micawber becomes clerk to Heep and, through exposing the frauds he has been perpetrating against Wickfield, foils him.

After Dora's death, David realises he loves Agnes, they marry and have at least five children.

David Copperfield locations feature in the following Walks 5,10,11 and 14.

Bleak House, 1853
Central to the novel is a long-running court case over inheritance, caused because several versions exist of a will, and known as Jarndyce vs Jarndyce. All the main characters stand to gain or lose, depending on which version of the will is upheld in the Chancery Court.

The kind-hearted John Jarndyce, beneficiary of one of the wills, takes in three wards: Esther Summerson (who provides one of the book's two narrative voices,) Richard Carstone and Ada Clare. The latter two are both beneficiaries of another of the contested wills. Esther, we discover, is secretly the illegitimate daughter of Lady Honoria Dedlock.

Richard and Ada fall in love and, while not forbidding them to marry, John Jarndyce insists that Richard first gain a profession. He fails to apply himself, coming to pin his hopes on landing an inheritance if the will that favours him is confirmed as the legitimate one. The action moves to Deal in Kent where Richard is stationed while attempting to forge a career in the army, and Ester comes to try to persuade him not to pin his hopes on a pay-out.

While in Deal, Esther spots Allan Woodcourt, who she was romantically involved with, but avoids him because smallpox has disfigured her once beautiful face. Woodcourt persists and asks Esther to marry him, but she is already engaged to her guardian, John Jarndyce. A further blow for Esther comes when Lady Dedlock dies while in great fear that her secret will be revealed to her husband. In the final pages of the book, Jarndyce frees Esther from her commitment to him, and she marries Woodcourt.

The legal case is settled, but costs have eaten up all the money.

Bleak House locations feature in Walk 15.

Great Expectations, 1861

The opening scene of young Pip confronted by the escaped convict Magwitch in a foggy churchyard on the Higham marshes is one of the most compelling in literature. Equally memorable is Pip's first meeting with Miss Havisham, an old lady abandoned at the altar who still wears her tattered wedding dress, and has stopped all the clocks in Satis House (Restoration House), her grand dwelling in Our Town (Rochester) at the minute she was spurned.

Pip, an orphan who lives with his sister and brother-in-law Joe Gargery, a blacksmith, at his forge on the marshes in real-life Lower Higham, is sent to Miss Haversham's, where he meets the haughty beauty Estella. Encountering riches, sophistication and beauty makes Pip ashamed of his humble background and lack of learning. When an anonymous benefactor pays for him to transfer to London, where he will be brought up as a gentleman, Pip is convinced Miss Havisham is his benefactor. However, it finally transpires that it is Magwitch he must thank.

Pip has been helplessly in love with Estella since their first meeting, and his heart is broken when she marries someone else. In a sequence of very Dickensian family connections, it transpires that Magwitch is Estella's father, and Compeyson, who escaped with Magwitch at the start of the book, is the swine who jilted Miss Havisham on her wedding day. In the final sequence, Magwitch turns up at Pip's lodgings. As someone who was transported for life, he faces death if captured, so Pip is determined to get him out of the country, taking him in a rowing boat down the Thames past Gravesend and the very marsh where he first encountered Magwitch. They are caught, Pip loses his source of income, and travels abroad to start a new life.

Eleven years later Pip returns and visits the ruins of Satis house where he meets the now-widowed Estella. She asks Pip to forgive her and he sees 'no shadow of another parting from her'.

Great Expectations locations feature in Walks 3,6 and 7.

The Uncommercial Traveller, 1861

Dickens wrote 17 essays in which he took on the persona of the Uncommercial Traveller. They were published from 1859 in his newly-founded journal *All The Year Round*, and in 1861 gathered into a book. At the time there were many who were known as Commercial Travellers; people who went from town to town trying to sell goods and services. Dickens felt an affinity for them, as a writer who travelled extensively, partly for pleasure, but mainly to observe and report on various aspects of Britain, Europe and America. Further essays followed over the rest of his life.

Dickens explained: 'I am both a town traveller and a country traveller, and am always on the road. Figuratively speaking, I travel for the great house of Human Interest Brothers, and have rather a large connection in the fancy goods way.'

The Uncommercial Traveller features in Walks 4 and 8.

The Mystery of Edwin Drood, 1870

Edwin Drood is an orphan living with his uncle, cathedral choir-master Jasper John, in a gatehouse in Cloisterham (Rochester). To fulfil a promise made to their now-dead fathers, he and Rosa Budd, also an orphan, intend to marry. Rosa is being educated at the Nun's House, based on Eastgate House in Rochester High Street.

Onto the scene come another pair of young orphans. Neville and Helena Landless are sent to live with Revd Septimus Crisparkle in Minor Canon Corner (based on Minor Canon Row).

Neville is immediately infatuated with Rosa, and a violent quarrel with Edwin Drood ensues.

When Edwin disappears, and his watch is found in the weir at the nearby river, suspicion falls on Neville, stoked by Jasper, an opium addict who also harbours a secret infatuation with Rosa.

Unknown to Jasper, Rosa and Edwin have decided they will not marry, but remain friends. Jasper only learns of this after Edwin's disappearance. When he does find out, his anguished reaction suggests that he might have had a hand in Edwin's disappearance.

That's as far as Dickens got with the novel, completing only six of the planned twelve episodes. Various theories have been propounded as to how he intended to continue the plot, but the truth is we simply don't know how he would have ended the novel.

Edwin Drood locations feature in Walks 4 and 8.

Bibliography

In writing this book, I have read or consulted the following books:

Ackroyd, Peter: *Dickens* (Sinclair-Stevenson, London, 1990)
Allbut, Robert: *Rambles in Dickens-Land* (Freemantle, London, 1899)
Bishop C H: *Charles Dickens in Folkestone* (privately published)
Forster, John: *The Life of Charles Dickens, Vols I – III* (Chapman and Hall, London, 1847)
Gadd, William: *The Great Expectations Country* (Cecil Palmer, London, 1929)
Harrison, Shirley and Evemy, Sally: *Dickens in Rochester* (S B Publications, Seaford, 1997)
Hughes, William R: *A Week's Tramp in Dickens-Land* (Chapman and Hall, London, 1891)
Langton, Robert: *The Childhood And Youth Of Charles Dickens* (Hutchinson, London, 1890)
Macaskill, Hilary: *Charles Dickens at Home* (Frances Lincoln, London, 2011)
Tomalin, Claire: *Charles Dickens: A Life* (Penguin, London, 2012)
Tomalin, Claire: *The Invisible Woman, The Story of Nelly Ternan and Charles Dickens* (Penguin, London, 1991)
Watts, Alan S: *Dickens At Gad's Hill* (Cedric Dickens and Elvendon Press, Goring-on-Thames, 1889)